KIDS

LOVE

INDIANA

A PARENT'S GUIDE TO EXPLORING FUN PLACES IN INDIANA WITH CHILDREN. . .YEAR ROUND!

GEORGE & MICHELE ZAVATSKY

KIDS LOVE PUBLICATIONS
7438 SAWMILL ROAD, SUITE 500
COLUMBUS, OH 43235

Dedicated to the Families of Indiana

KIDS ♥ INDIANA ™   Kids Love Publications

For the latest updates and information, visit our website:

www.kidslovepublications.com

Acknowledgements

We are most thankful to be blessed with our parents, Barbara Darrall and George and Catherine Zavatsky who helped us every way they could – typesetting, proofing and babysitting. More importantly, they were great sounding boards and offered loving, unconditional support.

We are thankful for the Starr Family who participated in the research. Toby Starr, Tony Starr, Nichole Starr, and our own Jenny Zavatsky have decorated our chapter cover pages with their illustrations. We are both thankful to them for their precious artwork. Our own young kids, Jenny and Daniel, were delightful and fun children during all of our trips across the state.

We both sincerely thank each other – our partnership has created a great "marriage of minds" with lots of exciting moments and laughs woven throughout.

Above all, we praise the Lord for His many answered prayers and special blessings throughout the completion of this project.

We think Indiana is a wonderful, friendly area of the country with more activities than you could imagine! Our sincere wish is that this book will help everyone "fall in love" with Indiana!

– *George & Michele*

INTRODUCTION

HOW TO USE THIS BOOK

If you are excited about discovering Indiana, this is the book for you and your family! Become a Hoosier State expert! We've spent over a thousand hours doing all the scouting, collecting and compiling (*and most often visiting!*) so that you could spend less time searching and more time having fun.

Here are a few hints to make your adventures run smoothly:

- ❑ Consider the **child's age** before deciding to take a visit.
- ❑ Know **directions** and parking. Call ahead if you have questions and bring this book. Also, don't forget your camera! *(please honor rules regarding use)*
- ❑ **Estimate the duration** of the trip. Bring small surprises (favorite juice boxes) and travel books and toys.
- ❑ Call ahead for **reservations** or details, if necessary.
- ❑ Most listings are **closed major holidays** unless noted.
- ❑ Make a **family "treasure chest"**. Decorate a big box or use an old popcorn tin. Store memorabilia from a fun outing, journals, pictures, brochures and souvenirs. Once a year, look through the "treasure chest" and reminisce.
- ❑ Plan **picnics** along the way. Many Historical Society sites and state parks are scattered throughout Indiana. Allow time for a rural/scenic route to take advantage of these free picnic facilities.
- ❑ Some activities, especially tours, require **groups** of 10 or more. To participate, you may either ask to be part of another tour group or get a group together yourself (neighbors, friends, school organizations). If you arrange a group outing most places offer discounts.

❑ Each chapter is listed by area (*see map below*), then by
city. **The front index lists places by 10 separate areas of
the state, the back index is alphabetical.**

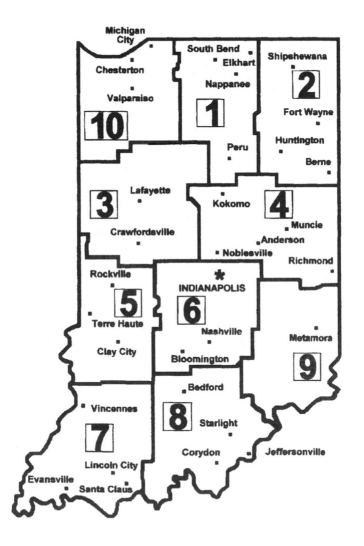

George Zavatsky and Michele (Darrall) Zavatsky were raised in the Midwest and have lived in several different cities throughout the region. Along with writing and self-publishing several books, each of them also own and operate a catalog marketing company and a courier business. Besides the wonderful adventure of marriage, they place great importance on being loving parents to Jenny and Daniel.

ATTRACTIONS & EVENTS (by area)

ATTRACTIONS & EVENTS (by area)

Area 2 *(listed by area, city, place/event, page #)*

ATTRACTIONS & EVENTS (by area)

Area 3 (listed by area, city, place/event, page #)

ATTRACTIONS & EVENTS (by area)

ATTRACTIONS & EVENTS (by area)

Area 5 *(listed by area, city, place/event, page #)*

ATTRACTIONS & EVENTS (by area)

Area 6 (listed by area, city, place/event, page #)

ATTRACTIONS & EVENTS (by area)

ATTRACTIONS & EVENTS (by area)

Area 7 *(listed by area, city, place/event, page #)*

ATTRACTIONS & EVENTS (by area)

ATTRACTIONS & EVENTS (by area)

Area 10 *(listed by area, city, place/event, page #)*

ATTRACTIONS & EVENTS (by area)

Table of Contents

Chapter 1

TOURS

BONNEYVILLE MILL

53373 CR 131 (2 ½ miles East on SR120 to CR 131 South), **Bristol**

- ❏ **Area: 1**
- ❏ Telephone Number: (219) 535-6458
- ❏ Hours: Daily, 10:00 am - 5:00 pm (May – October)
- ❏ Miscellaneous: Purchase freshly ground grains. Picnic area. Milling takes place on the half-hour.

S ee the oldest continually operating rustic gristmill in Elkhart County (1832). Grinds corn, wheat, buckwheat and rye using heavy milling stones. Freshly painted red mill and barn /gift shop is a delightful place to spend Lunch. Beautiful park and walking trails. Open year round.

RIVER QUEEN

Bowers Court on St. Joseph's River (Off Jackson Boulevard), **Elkhart**

- ❏ **Area: 1**
- ❏ Telephone Number: (219) 522-1795
- ❏ Hours: Sundays, 2:00 pm (May – October)
- ❏ Admission: General $5.00, Children $3.00 (2-12)
- ❏ Miscellaneous: Cruise up the St. Joseph River and learn fascinating facts about the river's history that dates back to 1841. Children like watching the ducks and other boats. At one time, the river was the only method of transportation.

DEUTSCH KASE HAUS
(pronounced "Doytch Case House")
CR 250 North (3 miles East of Middlebury),
Middlebury

- ❑ **Area: 1**
- ❑ Telephone Number: (219) 825-9511
- ❑ Hours: Monday - Friday, 8:00 am - 5:00 pm. Phone ahead to be sure they are making cheese each day.
- ❑ Tours: View easily through giant windows
- ❑ Miscellaneous: Retail shop also open Saturday, 8:00 am - 3:00 pm. Sample cheeses freshly made.

Making cheese is an art and this cheese haus takes no short cuts. They start with milk brought from Amish farms. The cows were milked the day before and the milk cooled in 10 gallon cans. Once at the cheese factory, the milk is pasteurized and placed in giant tubes where enzymes and flavors are added. Giant rotating stirrers (this is the favorite part to watch) separate the milk into whey and cheese curd. Later, the whey is drawn off and the remaining curd is salted and pressed. Our favorite cheese type they make is Colby - it really tastes better than any commercial brand (creamier, too!).

AMISH ACRES
1600 West Market Street (US 6. Off US 19), **Nappanee**

- ❑ **Area: 1**
- ❑ Telephone Number: (800) 800-4942 or (219) 773-4188
- ❑ Hours: Dawn to dusk, Monday -Saturday, 10:00 am - 6:00 pm. (March – December)
- ❑ Admission: Vary with attraction. $2.00 and up (each)
- ❑ Miscellaneous: Village shops open until 5:00 pm. The Round Barn Theater "Plain and Fancy" musical comedy

about Amish culture (a New York couple is mistakenly absorbed into Amish living) is a must!

After you watch "Beyond the Buggy" documentary film, tour a 122 year Amish homestead where the family still clings to simple dress and gentle farming. See chores and crafts of a typical Amish family including gardens, orchards and livestock. Now take a buggy ride and countryside tour. You'll have built up your appetite for the Thresher's Dinner at the Restaurant Barn. It's a thirteen item dinner full of family style food (our favorite is the first course including Sechler's pickles, apple butter and bean soup). If you're trying new foods, order shoofly pie for dessert (only if you LOVE the taste of molasses - our family opted for fruit pies).

SOUTH BEND CHOCOLATE COMPANY

3300 West Sample Street (just West of downtown. Off US 31), **South Bend**

- ❑ **Area: 1**
- ❑ Telephone Number: (800) 301-4961
- ❑ Admission: Free
- ❑ Tours: By appointment
- ❑ Miscellaneous: Exhibits and film of chocolate making process in Foyer. Free treat (bag full of goodies) at the end of the tour.

From the minute you walk up to the front door, you'll be surrounded with the smell of chocolate (they use cocoa bean shells as mulch in their plant beds outside!). Even the waiting area is fun with "chocolate-related" films playing (i.e. Willie Wonka) and little known facts like cocoa beans were once used as currency. The real fun treat before the tour is to adorn your complimentary white hair net and stand by a scaled-down conveyor just like the one Lucy and Ethel used (their picture with mouthfuls of candy is in the background). You must get a picture of this! The tour is simple and short and includes the "chocolate waterfall" and viewing a 10 lb. candy bar. As their sticker says, "You'll be sweeter since you visited South Bend Chocolate Company".

WARSAW CUT GLASS COMPANY
505 South Detroit Street, **Warsaw**

- ❑ **Area: 1**
- ❑ Telephone Number: (219) 267-6581
- ❑ Hours: Monday - Saturday, 9:00 am - 5:00 pm
- ❑ Admission: Free
- ❑ Tours: Of showroom and manufacturing facility during business hours. Watch cutting - 10:00 am or 2:00 pm (best times if group). No tours November and December.

Using turn-of-the century machinery, artisans hand cut pieces of clear crystal using techniques of the early 1900's. Stone wheels run with leather belts in a 1911 vintage workshop.

SEYFERT'S POTATO CHIPS AND PRETZELS
1001 Paramount Road, (I-69 to Exit 111A), **Fort Wayne**

- ❑ **Area: 2**
- ❑ Telephone Number: (219) 483-9521
- ❑ Admission: Free
- ❑ Tours: Maximum of 30 people. Tuesdays and Thursdays, 9:30 am - 3:00 pm. Lots of walking. Reservations required. 45 minutes.

Charles Seyfert started his company in 1934 in Fort Wayne after his potato chip samples became a hit at local saloons. Today, the plant produces 9000 lbs. of chips per hour and 100,000 twisted, baked pretzels each hour. Your guide is a spunky lady named Myrtle who has become an industry expert and odd potato chip shapes collector (she and her collection have appeared on the David Letterman Show). You'll get to see the best of her collection and hear potato chip stories at the beginning of the tour. Watch potatoes as they arrive in mounds, are dumped into bins and then sent to washers. After they are washed and scrubbed, they are mechanically peeled and sliced, then sent to cookers and salters. They take their final trip through a conveyor maze to be packaged. For every pound of raw potatoes, only about 3.2 oz. leave as chips. Sample bags of pretzels and chips are given away at the end of the tour.

AMISHVILLE USA
844 East 900 South (1-69 to Highway 218 to US 27 - Follow signs from Berne), Geneva

- ❑ **Area: 2**
- ❑ Telephone Number: (219) 589-3536
- ❑ Hours: Monday - Saturday, 9:00 am -5:00 pm. Sunday, 11:00 am - 5:00 pm. (April – December)
- ❑ Admission: Varies with activity
- ❑ Tours: Of Amish Home. Adults $2.75, Children $1.50 (6-12)
- ❑ Miscellaneous: Gift Shop. Essenplatz (eating place). Buggy rides of farm area, $1.25/person (ages 3+)

The tour of an Old Order Amish Home was the highlight of this visit. The guide includes the children in descriptions of a typical day - for instance, Sally would go fetch eggs while Johnny would milk cows or feed horses. A little girl or boy is chosen from the tour to be the "model" as they are adorned with different clothes to match their age (i.e. a young girl always wears her hair in two braids with no bangs with a bonnet and dress). Pins and occasional buttons are used in clothing - never shiny zippers. Young brides only change their outer apron for the wedding. See how families survive without electricity or plumbing and how close the families are (grandparents live in a house next to the main house). Set back on a country road lined with traditional Amish farms and buggies as people go about their daily chores. Truly authentic "Amish-cana"!

CLAY FACTORY
Third Street (off Main Street), **Grabill**

- ❑ **Area: 2**
- ❑ Telephone Number: (219) 627-3567
- ❑ Hours: Monday - Saturday, 9:00 - 5:00 pm. Sunday, Noon - 5:00 pm
- ❑ Tours: Afternoons best - Weekdays. By appointment only.

Country clay folk art made in a small workshop but shipped all over the world. They mostly make ornaments and country wall-hangings. Workers first design patterns and have a "stamp" or "cookie cutter" made of the new design. The clay is rolled out onto a slab and stamped or "cookie cut". Each piece is painted and fired in tub kilns. See if you can have your group "cut out" your favorite design.

GREENFIELD MILLS
1050 East 7560 North, **Howe**

- ❑ **Area: 2**
- ❑ Telephone Number: (219) 367-2394
- ❑ Hours: 8:00 am - 5:00 pm, Monday - Friday operations

- Admission: Adults $2.00, Children $0.50 (6-12)
- Tours: By appointment only
- Miscellaneous: Family-owned working mill since 1846. Hydroelectric generators now provide power to mill soft wheat flour.

MENNO-HOF, MENNONITE-AMISH VISITORS CENTER

510 South Van Buren Street (North of US 20 and SR 5), Shipshewana

- **Area: 2**
- Telephone Number: (219) 768-4117
- Hours: Monday - Saturday, 10:00 am   5:00 pm. (Adjusted seasonally)
- Admission: Donation. Suggested - Adults $4.00, Children $2.00
- Tours: One hour
- Miscellaneous: Most of the tour is "over the heads" of children twelve years and under; however, you can advise your guide of this and they can accommodate by spending significant time in the Interactive Room.

Where can you take one journey starting in a courtyard in 1525, in Europe, around a water pitcher? Then, get locked in a dungeon, escape in a cramped quarters ship, survive a tornado and learn about the power of faith! About halfway through, children will have the chance to walk around and play in an Amish built (beams, pegs and kneebraces only) barn stocked with simple wood toys. Our kids had to be pulled away - we may never buy "gadget" toys again! This is a very thorough walking tour of the story of tragedy and triumph of a people searching for peace. Afterwards, you'll truly understand the reasons for their way of life.

SECHLER'S FINE PICKLES

5686 SR 1 (1-69 North to DuPont Exit to SR 1 North - 20
miles), **St. Joe**

- ❑ **Area: 2**
- ❑ Telephone Number: (219) 337-5461
- ❑ Admission: Free
- ❑ Tours: Monday - Friday, 9-11:00 am & 1-3:00 pm
  (April – October)
- ❑ Miscellaneous: Because of insurance restrictions, children
  are restricted to view only from large windows. Retail
  showroom has sample table with one of each variety pickle
  available to taste. Try jalapeno slices, orange or candied
  raisin crispies.

Pucker up for pickles! Ralph Sechler began pickle processing in
1921 in his home (next to the factory). Pickles are just
cucumbers, salt, water, vinegar and spices but the secret
combination prepares just the right taste. Around the side of the
building, you might see truckloads of "cukes" arrive (farmers are
paid the highest price for "gherkins", the smallest) and sorted into
slots for seven different sizes. Each size is processed in covered
vats full of salt brine for 2½ months to 1½ years depending upon
demand. Before pickles are packaged, they are first cooked for 24
hours, then sliced, chopped or ground and left to marinate 1-10
days in special spice solutions. Workers stand by special stainless
steel tables and hand-pack each variety in its special brine. Our
favorite flavor is sweet apple cinnamon. Be sure to take some
home!

TWINROCKER HANDMADE PAPER
100 East Third, **Brookston**

☐ **Area: 3**
☐ Telephone Number: (765) 563-3119
☐ Hours: Monday - Friday, 9:00 am - 3:00 pm
☐ Admission: $4.00/person (1-11 people), $3.00/person (12+ people in group)
☐ Tours: By appointment. Ages 8+. Open tours at 1:30 pm Tuesdays.
☐ Miscellaneous: Tours can focus on the history of paper and writing materials.

The painstaking, lost art of making sheet paper by hand is back and Twinrocker was among the first hand mills to open in the 70's. Watch "cooked" cotton, husk or linen rag fibers turn into custom paper. You'll see them first beat the fiber with water which we learned releases cellulose causing fiber and water to bond. Next a mould or sieve is dipped into the vat of pulp and shaken. The new sheet formed is "couched" between pieces of wool felt, pressed and then dried. As the paper dries and water evaporates, the fibers bond closer. A special copywritten exaggerated "Feather" deckle edge is the company signature.

TOM ST. CLAIR STUDIO GLASS WORKSHOP
6360 Pendleton Avenue, **Anderson**

☐ **Area: 4**
☐ Telephone Number: (765) 642-7770
☐ Hours: Monday - Saturday, 10:00 am - 5:00 pm. Call first. Occasionally, he isn't firing and closes shop.
☐ Admission: Free

- ❑ Tours: Watch through large glass windows or pre-arrange a group tour.
- ❑ Miscellaneous: Hand-shaped molten glass. He makes paper weights, ornaments, perfume bottles and sculpture that are multi-colored and have an "air brush" look to them.

SCOTT SHAFER STONEWARE
610 North Morton Avenue, **Centerville**

- ❑ **Area: 4**
- ❑ Telephone Number: (765) 855-2409
- ❑ Hours: Monday - Saturday, 10:00 am - 5:00 pm
- ❑ Admission: Free
- ❑ Tours: 2 weeks notice. "Just come and ask questions while I work", says Scott
- ❑ Miscellaneous: Small Gift Shop/Showroom

Visit with Scott while he works by hand to create pottery with sound design and balance - meant to be used. He creates pitchers, stems, mugs, crocks, bowls and platters. He begins by making his own clay, wets it down; it's then hand-thrown and shaped on a potter's wheel. You'll be tempted to touch the wet clay which is glazed, painted and finally, heat dried. The pieces are dried using a brick kiln which is sealed each time for days. He must break the wall down to open it each time.

ABBOTT'S CANDY SHOP
48 East Walnut (I-70 to SR 1 to SR 38 [Left] to Perry [Left] to Walnut [Right]), **Hagerstown**

- ❑ **Area: 4**
- ❑ Telephone Number: (765) 489-4442

- ❑ Hours: Monday - Friday, 9:00 am - 5:00 pm. Candy Shop open Saturday, 9:00 am - 5:00 pm during Winter Holiday Season.
- ❑ Admission: Free
- ❑ Tours: Except Thanksgiving - Christmas. By appointment. 3rd grade+. Best before 11:30 am, not Lunch time
- ❑ Miscellaneous: 1st visit entitles you to one free sample of caramel wrapped right off the line.

Founded in the 1890's and still owned by the Abbott family members, they are nationally famous for their homemade caramels and chocolates made from 100 year old recipes. See the caramels made from scratch. First, butter is boiled in copper kettles and then milk and sugar are added. It was fun to hear the cook yell "CARAMEL!" just at the time it's finished cooking. The other ladies hurry over to help pour out the hot mixture on cold marble slabs. After it cools, the caramels are cut using a hand crank and each morsel is wrapped individually in white wax paper or sent over to the chocolate room for coating. You'll love their line of funny-named candies called Gismo, Gismae, Gisnut, Gishew and Gismond. Can you guess which nut belongs in each candy?

CARTHAGE, KNIGHTSTOWN AND SHIRLEY RAILROAD TRAIN

112 West Carey Street (I-70 to SR 109 Exit South Downtown), Knightstown

- ❑ **Area: 4**
- ❑ Telephone Number: (765) 345-5561; (800) 345-2704
- ❑ Hours: Friday - Sunday, Holidays, 10:30 am - 4:30 pm (May – October)
- ❑ Admission: Adults $6.00, Children $4.00 (3-11)
- ❑ Tours: 1 hour, 15 minutes round trip. Departure at 11:00 am, 1 & 3:00 pm.

❑   Miscellaneous: Quick stop in Carthage for a snack. Group
    rates 20+. Train Robbery trips in June and August. Gift
    Shop.

S it in the coach or caboose as it heads south passing under a
  railroad bridge and through the countryside. The covered
platform car (once part of a New York Central passenger and
freight station) serves as a spot to ride those in strollers or
wheelchairs. As the engine is "run around" for the return trip, you
can view rail equipment displays.

MICHAEL BOONE COPPERSMITH
103 East Main Street (I-70 to SR 109 to US 40E),
Knightstown

❑   **Area: 4**
❑   Telephone Number: (765) 345-7831
❑   Hours: Monday – Saturday, 9:00 am – 5:00 pm
❑   Admission: Free
❑   Tours: By appointment. School age. Monday - Friday only.
    (Minimum of 6 people)
❑   Miscellaneous: Showroom with copper treasures housed in
    a tin ceiling and pine floored old department store. Cookie
    cutters, trays, bowls, ornaments, etc.

A fter Michael had a serious disabling head injury in the early
  1980's, he needed a craft to occupy his time. His authentic
trendy and replica copper crafts caught attention. They are so well
known now, even Martha Stewart has a designer line that Mr.
Bonne's shop creates. On tour you will start at the beginning
seeing large sheets of copper cut, then curled or flattened, shaped
using all manual antique tools and finally soldered (attaching ends)
and scrubbed. The museum-style workshop is adapted from a 19th
century sheet metal shop. A "Santa's Workshop" atmosphere –

choose the "Hammer your own, hands on workshop" – for $1.00/person a coppersmith helps you create your own ornament. First choose from objects like ducks, angels, gingerbread men or stars. Next you're given a weathered hammer with one flat and one rounded end. Then, begin hammering your piece of copper over a wood block to your heart's delight! When you've achieved that "old colonial look" you can stop and hole punch the top. You now have a personalized souvenir for the tree – and the best souvenir of all – hand made.

KOKOMO OPALESCENT GLASS COMPANY
1310 South Market (Downtown), **Kokomo**

- ❑ **Area: 4**
- ❑ Telephone Number: (765) 457-8136
- ❑ Admission: Free
- ❑ Tours: Wednesday and Friday at 10:00 am or by appointment. No sandals. Parents must stay with children.
- ❑ Miscellaneous: Broken glass everywhere so follow guide's instructions carefully. Gift shop. We bought items with pink glass in it – especially after we understood it's value.

Dating back to 1888, it is the only remaining "Gas Boom" factory where up to 100 different types of glass are made for stained glass artisans. Four ingredients are used: flint, phosphorus, sand and opal – the combination is a secret known only by the owners. The 2600 degree furnaces run 365 days a year and 13 different roller patterns are used (some are custom to Tiffany). The process starts when the table guy rings the bell, the "ladlers" use giant ladles to scoop out different colored molten glass and spoon it onto the table where it's mixed with a giant fork. Next the blob is rolled, slowly cooled and then cut. A pink color is most expensive because it contains some 24K gold. Red, orange and yellow are second most expensive because they contain arsenic (which is expensive to ventilate) during production.

INDIANA TRANSPORTATION MUSEUM
325 Cicero Road (Forest Park and I-19), **Noblesville**

- ❑ **Area: 4**
- ❑ Telephone Number: (317) 773 – 6000
- ❑ Hours: Tuesday - Sunday, 10:00 am - 5:00 pm. (Memorial Day - Labor Day) Weekends only. (April, May, September, October)
- ❑ Admission: Adults $3.00, Children $2.00 (4-12)
- ❑ Miscellaneous: Train rides additional charge.

R ide to the Indiana State Fair or just a simple tour on an authentic steam or diesel train. Tour 50 rail cars with antics and stories from retired railroad volunteers. Trolley tours daily (1920's era cars). Artifacts displayed within train cars.

THE "GIANT" EARTH HOME
2928 West Larry Street. (Meet at Faulk Park for tours).
Pendleton

- ❑ **Area: 4**
- ❑ Telephone Number: (765) 778-2757
- ❑ Hours: Reservations only
- ❑ Admission: Adults $6.00, Students $4.00
- ❑ Tours: Ages 5+

A do-it-yourself home in the woods built by local, Vic Cook. Powered by solar energy and full of environmental science equipment. Made with available materials of stone and scavenged wood. The kids' most intriguing part is the refrigerator built out of a hollowed birch log using high tech science to keep it cool.

CLAY CITY POTTERY
Corner of SR 156 South and 14th Street, **Clay City**

- ❑ **Area: 5**
- ❑ Telephone Number: (800) 776-2596
- ❑ Hours: Monday - Friday, 8:00 am - 4:00 pm, Saturday, 8:00 am – Noon.
- ❑ Admission: Free
- ❑ Tours: Pre-arranged
- ❑ Miscellaneous: Pottery Festival 2nd weekend in June. (812) 448-8457

Table-safe stoneware produced by a pottery factory. Owned by the 4th generation of the Griffith family. They are the only working commercial stoneware potters in Indiana. The hand-jiggered process of molding (pressing out water) is a very interesting manufacturing step; however, the kids seem to like the raw clay best. The large conveyor drying kilns keep things warm - we recommend tours in tempered weather seasons.

INDIANAPOLIS HORSE-DRAWN CARRIAGE RIDES
Downtown, **Indianapolis**

- ❑ **Area: 6**
- ❑ Miscellaneous: Average $30.00/ride for up to 4 people on a 30 minute ride. Reservations accepted. Usually parked in front of major downtown hotels and Circle Centre Mall.
  - • Colonial Carriage (317) 637-2004

- Metropolitan Carriage Co. (317) 631-4169
- Yellow Rose Carriage (317) 634-3400

INDIANAPOLIS MOTOR SPEEDWAY
4790 West 16th Street, **Indianapolis**

- ❑ **Area: 6**
- ❑ Telephone Number: (317) 484-6747
- ❑ Hours: Daily 9:00 am – 5:00 pm (except Christmas Day)
- ❑ Admission: General Admission $3 track tour, $3 museum (ages 16 and under free)
- ❑ Tours: By mini-bus, weather permitting
- ❑ Miscellaneous: Gift shop. Home of the Indy 500 and the NASCAR Brickyard 400.

Drive right onto the inside track as you are awed by the size of the speedway. Built initially as a proving ground for autos, it developed into the largest one day sporting event in the world and the greatest spectacle in racing – the Indy 500. The Hall of Fame Museum contains over 75 vehicles and numerous artifacts and trivia videos. Antique motorized vehicles, race winning cars, pace cars and even a rocket – boosted car can be seen. Stop in the theatre to view a film of race highlights. Maybe the best part of your visit will be the racetrack bus tour. Adrenaline is pumping as you make one lap with a narrative around each turn. There is nothing like the view as you approach the first turn – scary normally, but comforting to know the bus is only going 35 mph! The start/finish line has one strip of the original brick track. The black and white checkered victory circle actually raises the winning car and driver high into the air so all spectators can see. You'll also get a view of Gasoline Alley where drivers and mechanics spend pre-race time pampering their cars. The gift shop has no trouble selling souvenirs to the starry-eyed visitors who can only dream of such speed.

INDIANA STATE POLICE YOUTH EDUCATION AND HISTORICAL CENTER

8500 East 21st Street (Off 1-70), Indianapolis

- ❏ **Area: 6**
- ❏ Telephone Number: (317) 899-8293. (888) 477-9688
- ❏ Hours: Monday - Friday, 8 - 11:00 am and 1 - 4:00 pm. 1st and 3rd Saturday, 9:00 am - 4:00 pm
- ❏ Admission: Donation
- ❏ Tours: Groups by appointment

To teach respect for the police force or to pretend to be an officer for awhile – here's the place to go. Police vehicles are everywhere - restored classics, miniature police cars from every state or you can sit in a real car (turn on lights, sirens or intercom radio). Also, see displays and firearms; exhibit of Indiana's own John Dillinger; or bicycle safety.

RCA DOME

100 South Capitol Avenue, Indianapolis

- ❏ **Area: 6**
- ❏ Telephone Number: (317) 237-DOME
- ❏ Hours: Monday - Saturday at 11:00 am, 1 & 3:00 pm. Sunday at 1 & 3:00 pm. (March – November)
- ❏ Admission: Adults $5.00, Seniors $4.00 (55+), Children $ 4.00 (5-17)

The air supported dome stadium is 95,000 square feet and seats 60,500. The tours of the home of the Indy Colts include technical and fun, behind-the-scenes facts. Your tour begins at City Center with a multi-media presentation that includes lasers and confetti. Learn how the roof is self-cleaning (secret is Teflon-coated fiberglass) and takes up 8 acres with 2 miles of steel cable. The best part is seeing the Locker Rooms (famous players, first aid, work-out facilities), VIP suites and the Press Box. You even get to venture to the edge of the field!

MADAME C. J. WALKER THEATRE CENTER

617 Indiana Avenue (A few blocks from White River Park), **Indianapolis**

- ❑ **Area: 6**
- ❑ Telephone Number: (317) 236-2099
- ❑ Hours: Monday, Wednesday, Thursday, Friday, 9:00 am – 5:00 pm, Tuesday, 11:00 am – 5 :00 pm
- ❑ Admission: Free
- ❑ Tours: By appointment. 30 minutes

B ecause Madame Walker worked long hours and ate poorly, she began losing her hair. Frustrated, she cooked up different ingredients in her kitchen trying to find a solution that would make hair grow full and healthy. When she found a combination, neighbors began asking for some. Soon, she was advertising in newspapers and filling orders by mail. Madame created a line of shampoo, hair grower and oil treatments and began the first cosmetic direct sales. Known as the nation's 1st woman millionaire, the Center is a restoration of the former 1920's headquarters of her cosmetic business. Now it is a cultural showcase for the city's African American community. The theatre is decorated with African motif from collections of journeys to Africa.

ALEXANDER'S CARRIAGE RIDES
Franklin and VanBuren Streets, **Nashville**

- **Area: 6**
- Telephone Number: (812) 988-8230
- Hours: Daily, weather permitting
- Tours: Horse-drawn carriage rides with Tim, the driver and his horse, Dan
- Miscellaneous: Interesting sites are pointed out throughout downtown.

EAST FORK LIVERY CARRIAGE RIDES
Franklin and VanBuren Streets, **Nashville**

- **Area: 6**
- Telephone number: (812) 988-1143
- Hours: Daily, weather permitting
- Tours: Horse-drawn carriage rides through downtown
- Miscellaneous: Photos available upon request.

NASHVILLE EXPRESS TRAIN TOURS
Franklin and Van Buren Streets, **Nashville**

- **Area: 6**
- Telephone Number: (812) 988-2308
- Hours: Daily, 10:00 am - 8:00 pm (April – October)
- Admission: $4.00 (ages 5+)
- Tours: 2.5 mile narrated tour of downtown. Pickup at major motels every 20 minutes.
- Miscellaneous: Simulated steam locomotive train.

GRAHAM FARMS CHEESE
Highway 57 North, **Elnora**

☐ **Area: 7**
☐ Telephone Number: (800) 472-9178
☐ Hours: Monday – Saturday, 8:00 am – 6:00 pm, Sunday, Noon – 5:00 pm
☐ Tours: Monday – Friday (early in day)
☐ Miscellaneous: View cheesemaking (they've been making it since 1928). Cheese sampling. Ask how early Amish farmers brought their raw milk in the morning. Purdue and State of Indiana cheeses are a must souvenir.

TURNER DOLL FACTORY
RR 1, Heltonville - Bartlettsville Road (Highway 50 East to 446 North to Highway 58 [Left], [Right, off 58 at school], Follow signs), **Bedford**

☐ **Area: 8**
☐ Telephone Number: (812) 834-6692; (800) 887-6372
☐ Hours: Monday - Friday, 8:00 am - 5:00 pm. Saturday, 10:00 - 3:00 pm
☐ Admission: Free
☐ Tours: Monday - Friday until 3:00 pm
☐ Miscellaneous: Gift Shop with over-run discounted dolls. Located on farm property so the non-doll lovers can wander outside to see the variety of animals. They will send you a map to the exact location of property.

How are dolls' eyes popped in? This, and many questions you wouldn't even think to ask are answered during this delightfully explained tour. The vinyl parts of a doll are made with liquid that looks like thick, light chocolate milk. Liquid vinyl is poured into the mold of a head, arm or leg and then put in a rotating oven. How do they get the vinyl to coat just the outside of the mold and not fill the inside? Artists hand-paint the faces and add accents of blush (with an airbrush) to certain parts of the arms and legs to make them look real. Next, the doll is assembled and stuffed with "fluff" and beads in just the right places so when you hold the baby doll, it feels real! Each doll has its own name and outfit (hand-sewn by locals) . Our favorite is the "Kradle Kids" collection - they have such cute "pouty faces".

CORYDON SCENIC RAILROAD

210 West Walnut (and Water Street), **Corydon**

- ❑ **Area: 8**
- ❑ Telephone Number: (812) 738-8000
- ❑ Hours: Wednesday - Sunday, (Mid-June - Mid-August) Weekends only, (late May – September, October and early November)
- ❑ Admission: Adults $9.00, Seniors $1.00 off, Children $5.00 (4+)
- ❑ Tours: 1:00 pm weekdays, 1 & 3:00 pm, weekends and holidays. 1 ½ hour ride.
- ❑ Miscellaneous: Group tours 30+. Air-conditioned. Train depot - memorabilia and snacks.

All aboard the Silverliner train. The 115 year old railroad passes by the history of 1820's Corydon on 16 miles of track in the Indiana countryside.

ZIMMERMAN ART GLASS COMPANY

395 Valley Road (Exit 105 to Hwy 135 South and Hwy 337 to SR 62 to Mulberry to Valley Road), **Corydon**

- **Area: 8**
- Telephone Number: (812) 738-2206
- Hours: Tuesday – Saturday, 9:00 am – 4:30 pm
- Admission: Free
- Tours: 30 minute demos, Tuesday – Friday only 10:00 am – 1:00 pm or 2 – 4:00 pm.
- Miscellaneous: Recently produced and signed art glass pieces available on site for purchase – you just have to wait until they finish the piece they're working on.

Generations old and world renowned glass artisans make hand-blown glass paperweights, lamps, bowls and bottles. Two brothers work in a small workshop in an authentic workspace so small that you can stand close to the artist. Watch as they get a glob of premixed colored molten glass and, by constantly twirling it on a long stick, begin to use old world tools to shape the "glob" into their signature "flower". After a few cycles of heating/shaping/cooling the flower they let it "twirl cool" to make the final paperweight with a blossomed flower inside. You have to see this remarkable process. Our group was speechless and mesmerized to the point that we didn't even ask questions.

INDIANA RAILWAY MUSEUM AND TRAIN RIDES
Route 56, **French Lick**

- **Area: 8**
- Telephone Number: (800) 74-TRAIN
- Hours: Weekends, 10:00 am, 1 & 4:00 pm (April – October)
- Admission: Adults $8.00, Children $4.00 (3-11) Groups: (15+)
- Tours: 1¾ hour train trip

❑   Miscellaneous: Train Robbery Rides on Memorial Day,
      July 4th and Labor Day weekends. Gift Shop and snacks.

The museum displays diesel and steam locomotives, a rare
railway Post Office car and a 1951 dining car. The Springs
Valley Electric Trolley (shortest trolley line in the world) carries
passengers from French Lick to West Baden. Take the Train Ride
through 20 miles of Hoosier National Forest and the 2200 ft.
Burton Tunnel (one of the longest railroad tunnels in the state).
The area's history is related by uniformed crew members - many
who have personal stories to tell.

FOREST DISCOVERY CENTER

533 Louis Smith Road (I – 64 exit 119. Follow signs for
Hubers), **Starlight**

❑   **Area: 8**
❑   Telephone Number: (812) 923-1590
❑   Hours: Monday – Saturday, 9:00 am – 5:00 pm.
      Sunday, 1 – 6:00 pm
❑   Admission: Adults $5.50, Seniors $4.50 (55+), Children
      $3.00 (6 –12)
❑   Tours: Every ½ hour
❑   Miscellaneous: Gift shop with wood artwork, toys,
      souvenirs.

As you enter from the lobby you'll explore the unique indoor
forest made from wood products and complete with forest
sounds (birds, brush). Upstairs you can walk through an enormous
giant oak tree where you can view videos and sign the tree in
support of re-forestation efforts. Next, gaze at the 1000 sq. ft.
mural created from small wood inlays using age-old techniques
called "marquetry". Artisans are usually available to show you
how it was done. A glass enclosed skywalk brings you to Koetter

Woodworkings rough mill. Arrows and signs describe how logs become trimmed and molded. They don't waste anything...even the sawdust left over is burned as fuel for the electric generators. Defective wood chunks are made into mulch. The 13 step process begins with sawed logs, then dried in kilns to remove moisture, then planed, then electronically cut and finally jointed or sorted by size of "clear" (non-defective) board.

OHIO RIVER CRUISES/DOTTIE G. RIVERBOAT
Aurora Riverfront, **Aurora**

- **Area: 9**
- Telephone Number: (888) DOTTIE-G
- Hours: End of April - October
- Admission: Yes
- Miscellaneous: Café. 149 passenger authentic wheeler.

WHITEWATER VALLEY RAILROAD
SR 121 off SR 1 South (Downtown), **Connersville**

- **Area: 9**
- Telephone Number: (765) 825-2054
- Hours: Saturdays, Sundays, Holidays at Noon, (May – October)
- Admission: Adults $12.00, Children $6.00 (2-12)
- Tours: Start at Noon. 2 hour stop, returns at 6:00 pm. Early train (10:00 am) in October
- Miscellaneous: Bring a sack lunch to eat while on the train. Sit-down meals in stop at Metamora. Gift Shop with extensive "Thomas The Train" items.

HISTORIC RISING SUN OPEN-AIR TROLLEY

Central downtown, **Rising Sun**

- ❑ **Area: 9**
- ❑ Telephone Number: (888) RSNG-SUN
- ❑ Hours: Weekends, (May – October)
- ❑ Admission: Yes
- ❑ Tours: 25 minutes of historic rivertown.

WOOD'S HISTORIC GRIST MILL

9410 Old Lincoln Highway (in Deep River County Park), **Hobart**

- ❑ **Area: 10**
- ❑ Telephone Number: (219) 769-9030 or (219) 947-1958
- ❑ Hours: Daily, 10:00 am - 5:00 pm (May – October)
- ❑ Admission: Free
- ❑ Miscellaneous: General Store - old fashioned wooden floors, jars of candy and sundries.

Restored late 1800's mill designed to expose you to the process of a gristmill and pioneer life. The first floor is where the raw grain is ground by large stones. The other two floors are displays of period settings. Also take a peek in the 1830's sawmill.

Check out these businesses / services in your area for tour ideas:

AIRPORTS

Understand all the jobs it takes to run an airport. Tour the terminal, baggage claim, gates and security / currency exchange. Maybe you'll even get to board a plane.

ANIMAL SHELTERS

Great for the would-be pet owner.

BANKS

Take a "behind the scenes" look at automated teller machines, bank vaults and drive-thru window chutes. You may want to take this tour and then open a savings account for your child.

ELECTRIC COMPANY / POWER PLANTS

Coal furnaces heat water, which produces steam, that propels turbines, that drive generators, that make electricity.

FIRE STATIONS

Many Open Houses in October, Fire Prevention Month. Take a look into the life of the firefighters servicing your area and try on their gear. See where they hang out, sleep and eat.

HOSPITALS

Some Children's Hospitals offer pre-surgery and general tours.

NEWSPAPERS

You'll be amazed at all the new technology. See monster printers and robotics. See samples in the layout department and maybe try to put together your own page. National Newspaper Week is in October.

RESTAURANTS

DOMINO'S PIZZA

❑   Various locations

Telephone your local shop for tour status. Free. Usually ages
4+.   Takes 15 – 20 minutes.   Your children can be pizza
bakers!   While the group is instructed on ingredients and pizza
secrets, they will get to make their own special pizza.   After the
custom made pizza bakes, your tour guide will take it out of the
special oven, box it up and you get to take it home.

PIZZA HUT

❑   Many participating restaurants

Telephone the store manager. Best days are Monday, Tuesday
and Wednesday mid-afternoon.   Minimum of 10 people.
$3.50 per person. All children love pizza – especially when they
can create their own! As the children tour the kitchen, they learn
how to make a pizza, bake it, and then eat it.   The admission
charge includes lots of creatively make pizzas, beverage and
coloring book.

MCDONALD'S RESTAURANTS

❑   Participating locations

Telephone the store manager. They prefer Monday or Tuesday.
Free.   What child doesn't love McDonald's food?   This is
your child's chance to go behind the counter and look at the
machines that make all the fun food.   You will be shown the
freezer and it's alarm, the fryer and hamburger flipping on the
grills. There is a free snack at the end of the tour.

SUPERMARKETS

Kids are fascinated to go behind the scenes of the same store where Mom and Dad shop. Usually you will see them grind meat, walk into large freezer rooms, watch cakes and bread bake and receive free samples along the way. Maybe you'll even get to pet a live lobster!

TV/ RADIO STATIONS

Studios, newsrooms, Fox kids clubs. Why do weathermen never wear blue clothes on TV?

WATER TREATMENT PLANTS

A giant science experiment! You can watch seven stages of water treatment. The favorite is usually the wall of bright buttons flashing as workers monitor the different processes.

US MAIN POST OFFICES

Did you know Ben Franklin was the first Postmaster General (over 200 years ago)? Most interesting is the high-speed automated mail processing equipment. Learn how to address envelopes so they will be sent quicker (there are secrets). To make your tour more interesting, have your children write a letter to themselves and address it with colorful markers. Mail it earlier that day and they will stay interested trying to locate their letter in all the high-speed machinery.

COLLEGES

UNIVERSITY OF NOTRE DAME

1 – South Bend. (219) 239-7367. 1250 acre mystical campus founded in 1842 with notable landmarks like the Snite Museum of Art, the "Golden Dome", the Grotto and Log Chapel. Be sure to include the "Fighting Irish" football grounds and a snack at "The Huddle" food court. (Mid-May to Mid-August)

PURDUE UNIVERSITY

3 – Lafayette. Visitor Information Center, 504 Northwestern Avenue. (765) 494-INFO. Self-guided walking tour or student guided tours. Memorial Union student hangout, Fountains (one with goldfish), Horticulture Park, Library and Big Ten Sports Arenas and Stadiums.

INDIANA WESLEYAN UNIVERSITY

4 – Marion. (317) 674-6901. Roman Gothic style buildings, museum of Indian artifacts and fossil collections.

INDIANA STATE UNIVERSITY

5 – Terre Haute. Downtown. Anthropology museum and astronomical observatory. Intercollegiate sports with past attendees like Larry Bird (basketball), Kurt Thomas (gymnast) and Bruce Baumgartner (Olympic gold medal wrestler).

INDIANA UNIVERSITY

6 – Bloomington. East Seventh Street. (800) 209-8145. Indiana Memorial Union – largest student union with hotel and shopping mall inside. Jordan Hall Greenhouse, Kirkwood Observatory, Memorial Stadium Athletic Complex (Hoosier basketball and football), Metz Carillon Tower, Lilly Library, Art Museums. Showalter Fountain was designed by Ralph Laurent. Well House – drinking fountains and frequent site of a "Freshman Kiss". Indiana Indian modern art sculpture.

VINCENNES UNIVERSITY

7 – Jasper. Hwy. 162. (812) 968-4578. Indiana Baseball Hall of Fame. High school, college and pro players that called themselves "Hoosier" breed. Student Center.

Chapter 2

SEASONAL &
SPECIAL EVENTS

YEAR LONG

PIONEER DAYS / ENCAMPMENTS

E arly 1800's frontier life. Period costumed townsfolk, soldiers, Native Americans. See fur trading posts, kids' infantry, barber shop medicine, and old-fashioned games. Demonstrations of spinning, broom making, dancing, weaving, woodcarving, blacksmiths and tomahawk throwing. Open hearth cooking with period foods for sale like kettle popcorn and chips, cider, stew, barbecue, buffalo burgers, dumplings, apple butter, ham & beans, birch tea and Indian fry bread.

APRIL (late)

REDBUD TRAIL RENDEZVOUS

1 – **Rochester**. Fulton County Historical Society Grounds. (219) 223-4436.

MOUNTAIN MEN RENDEZVOUS

5 – **Bridgeton**. (765) 548-2136. No Admission.

MAY

SQUIRREL VILLAGE FESTIVAL

1 – **Bunker Hill**. 200W & 650S. (800) 346-6074. No Admission. (1st weekend)

TRADER DAYS

1 – **Oswego**. Campgrounds. (219) 594-2822. Admission. (3rd weekend)

FESTIVAL OF THE WHIPPOORWILL MOON

2 – **Huntington**. Forks of the Wabash Park. (219) 356-1903. (1st weekend)

COLONIAL HIGHLAND GATHERING

5 – Terre Haute. Fowler Park. (812) 232-3566. No Admission. (2nd weekend)

WESSELMAN WOODS NATURE PRESERVE

7 – Evansville. (812) 479-0771. (1st weekend)

SPIRIT OF VINCENNES RENDEZVOUS

7 – Vincennes. French Commons. Battlefield activities of George Rogers Clark. Admission. (Memorial Day weekend)

VOYAGEURS RENDEZVOUS

10 – Hebron. Grand Kankawee Marsh County Park. (219) 769-PARK. Admission. (3rd weekend)

JUNE

FEAST OF THE WILD ROSE MOON

1 – Middlebury. (800) 517-9739. (1st weekend)

ROUND BARN RENDEZVOUS

1 – Rochester. Fulton County Historical Society grounds. US 31. (219) 223-4436. No Admission. (2nd weekend)

CIVIL WAR DAYS

5 – Rockville. Billie Creek Village. (765) 569-3430. Admission. (2nd weekend)

CIVIL WAR DAYS

10 – Lowell. Buckley Homestead County Park. (219) 696-0769. Admission. (3rd weekend)

AUGUST

PIONEER LIVING HISTORY FESTIVAL

2 – **LaGrange**. David Rogers Park. (219) 463-4022. Admission. (Late in the month)

RODGERS RANGERS RENDEZVOUS

3 – **Cutler**. Adams Mill. (765) 463-7893. French- Indian War. No Admission. (Late in the month)

SKINNER FARM MUSEUM & VILLAGE

5 – **Perrysville**. SR32W. (765) 793-4079. Admission. (3rd weekend)

CIVIL WAR RE-ENACTMENT

9 – **Aurora**. US 50. (812) 744-3288. Relive Morgan's raid through Dearborn County. No Admission. (3rd weekend)

SEPTEMBER

BONNEYVILLE MILL

1 – **Bristol**. (800) 517-9739. (3rd weekend)

BACK TO THE DAYS OF KOSCIUSZKO

1 – **Warsaw**. Lucerne Park. (219) 267-2012. Admission. (Last weekend)

JOHNNY APPLESEED FESTIVAL

2 – **Fort Wayne**. Johnny Appleseed Park. (219) 497-6000. Celebrate the life and times of John Chapman. 100,000 attendance. (3rd weekend)

FORKS OF THE WABASH PIONEER FESTIVAL

2 – **Huntington**. Olde Towne. (800) 848-4282. Admission. (Last weekend)

BUCKSKINNERS RENDEZVOUS

3 – **Cutler**. Adams Mill. (765) 463-7893. Admission. (Last Saturday)

CIVIL WAR ENCAMPMENT

4 – **Cambridge City**. Huddleston Farmhouse Inn. (765) 478-3172. Admission. (Weekend after Labor Day)

WAYNE COUNTY HISTORICAL MUSEUM

4 – **Richmond**. (765) 962-5756. Admission. (2nd weekend)

TRAIL OF COURAGE LIVING HISTORY FESTIVAL

5 – **Rochester**. (219) 223-4436. Honor Potawatomi family as county's original inhabitants. Admission.

HERITAGE DAYS

6 – **Indianapolis**. Robin Run Village. (317) 293-5500. No Admission. (3rd Saturday)

CIVIL WAR DAYS & BATTLE

6 – **Mooresville**. Pioneer Park. (765) 831-7149. (Weekend after Labor Day)

COUNCIL GROUND GATHERING

7 – **Vincennes**. Indiana Territory State Historic Site. (812) 882-7422. No Admission. (Labor Day weekend)

OLD SETTLERS DAYS

8 – **Salem**. Steven's Memorial Museum. (812) 883-4500. (Mid-month)

FRONTIER DAYS RENDEZVOUS

9 – **Dunlapsville**. Treaty-Line Pioneer Village & Museum. (765) 855-5681. Admission. (Labor Day weekend)

SEPTEMBER (cont.)

FRONTIER DAYS

10 – LaPorte. Creek Ridge County Park. (219) 324-5855. Admission. (Last weekend)

DUNELAND HARVEST FESTIVAL

10 – Porter. Chellberg Farm & Bailly Homestead. (219) 926-7561. No Admission. (3rd weekend)

OCTOBER

SQUIRREL VILLAGE FESTIVAL

1 – Bunker Hill. 200W & 650S. (800) 346-6074. No Admission. (1st weekend)

CIVIL WAR DAYS & LIVING HISTORY

2 – Hartford City. SR 26. (765) 348-3200. Also tour a medical training school. Admission. (2nd weekend)

FEAST OF THE HUNTER'S MOON

3 – Lafayette. Fort Quiatenon Historic Park. (765) 476-8402. Admission. (2nd weekend)

MISSISSINEWA 1812

4 – Marion. Battlefield. (800) 822-1812. Largest War of 1812 living history event in the U.S. with average attendance of 30,000. Admission.

PIONEER DAYS

5 – Terre Haute. Fowler Park. (812) 462-3391. No Admission. (1st weekend)

CIVIL WAR RE-ENACTMENT

7 – Loogootee. West Boggs Park. (812) 295-3421. Admission. (1st weekend)

AUTUMN ON THE RIVER

8 – **Bethlehem**. Town Commons. (812) 256-6111. Recreation of founding of Bethlehem in 1812. No Admission. (3rd weekend)

REBIRTH OF THE BUFFALO

8 – **Elizabeth**. Needmore Buffalo Farm. (800) 752-4766. Tours of farm and buffalo food. (2nd weekend)

FT. VALLONIA DAYS

8 – **Vallonia**. (888) 524-1914. Reconstructed fort/tepees. No Admission. (3rd weekend)

LANIER DAYS SOCIAL

9 – **Madison**. Lanier Mansion. (812) 265-3526. No Admission. (2nd Saturday)

BUCKLEY HOMESTEAD DAYS

10 – **Lowell**. (219) 696-0769. Admission. (1st weekend)

JANUARY

KIDSFEST

6 – **Indianapolis**. RCA Dome. (317) 262-3452. Hands-on kid and family activities in arts, sports, education and recreation. Over 100 exhibitors showcase kids' products. Admission - over age 2.

WINTERFEST

10 – **LaPorte**. City and County Parks, Mall. (219) 326-8115. Sleigh rally, sleigh rides, snowmobile races, winter fishing, snowball volleyball and softball, ice sculptures, snowman contest. No Admission. (Last weekend)

FEBRUARY

WINTERFEST

2 – Huntington. Little Turtle Recreation Area. (219) 468-2165. Sled dog demo runs, outdoor skills activities like cooking and survival skills for camping. No Admission. (2nd Saturday)

JAMES DEAN BIRTHDAY CELEBRATION

4 – Fairmount. Historical Museum. (765) 948-4555. Dean's childhood home, authentic exhibits at museum and James Dean Gallery, free film showings, cake and punch. No Admission. (2nd weekend)

FEBRUARY / MARCH

MAPLE SYRUP FESTIVALS

Learn how maple syrup is made from tree tapping to evaporator demonstrations. Taste sampling of food with syrup like pancakes and kettle popcorn. Pioneer music and games.

- ❑ **1 – Wakarusa**. Downtown. (219) 862-4344. No Admission. (Last Friday / Saturday of March)
- ❑ **2 – LaGrange**. Maplewood Nature Center. (219) 463-4022. No Admission. (3rd weekend in March)
- ❑ **5 – Rockville**. Parke County Fairgrounds and Billie Creek Village. (765) 569-5226. Some Admission. (Last two weekends of February)
- ❑ **5 – Terre Haute**. Prairie Creek Park. (812) 462-3391. No Admission. (Month-long February)
- ❑ **7 - Evansville**. Wesselman Woods Nature Preserve. (812) 479-0771. Admission. (Early March weekend)
- ❑ **8 – Salem**. Sugarbush Farm. (812) 967-4491. No Admission. (1st two weekends in March)

❑   **10 – Porter.** Chellberg Farm & Bailly Homestead. (219) 926-7561. (1st two weekends in March)

MARCH

ST. PATRICK'S DAY CELEBRATIONS

On or the week before St. Patrick's Day see a downtown lunchtime parade. "Wearin of the green" celebrations include Irish Dancing, food and music. No Admission.

❑   Participating towns: **Indianapolis, Ireland, South Bend.**

APRIL

EASTER EGG HUNTS

Egg hunts, party with Easter Bunny, egg decorating contests, Easter Bonnet contests. No Admission.

❑   Participating towns: **5 – Cloverdale Eagles Mill Lake (765) 795-4576; 5 – Terre Haute Deming Park (812) 298-talk; 6 – Indianapolis Parks & Rec. (317) 327-0000; 9 – Vevay (800) HELLO-VV.**

INTERNATIONAL FOOD BAZAAR

3 – **West Lafayette.** University Church. (765) 743-4353. Authentic foods from over 25 different countries, cultural displays and dress. No Admission. (Mid-month Saturday)

EARTH DAY – ARBORFEST

4 - **Anderson.** Geater Community Center. (765) 648-6853. Earth-friendly activities, tree giveaways and plantings. No Admission. (Last Saturday)

APRIL (cont.)

MOREL MADNESS

9 – **Metamora**. Trappers Rendezvous on Canal Street. (765) 698-1245. Prizes for the largest or most morels brought in. Mushroom tastings, greased pig contest, chicken hypnotizing. No Admission, except for contest entry fees. (Last weekend of April / 1st weekend of May)

MAY

THE 500 FESTIVALS (Activities to celebrate the Indy 500 Race)

ANDERSON LITTLE 500 FESTIVAL & RACE

❑   4 – **Anderson**. Various locations. (765) 640-2457. Big wheel race, concert, fireworks, sprint car race. No Admission. (Month-long)

BANK ONE FESTIVAL & KIDS DAY

❑   6 – **Indianapolis**. Monument Circle. (800) 638-4296. The city's largest outdoor festival for children with Big Wheel races (ages 2-5), carnival, arts and crafts, prizes. No Admission. except for race registrants. (Second Saturday)

500 FESTIVAL COMMUNITY DAY

❑   6 – **Indianapolis**. Motor Speedway. (800) 638-4296. Lap the track in your own vehicle. See Pit Row, Gasoline Alley, and the Tower Terrace. Driver's and mechanic's autographs. Admission. (Thursday before race)

500 FESTIVAL PARADE

❑   **6 – Indianapolis.** Downtown. (800) 638-4296. Drivers, floats, marching bands, celebrities. Admission for reserved seating. (Noon the day before race)

LILLY 500 FESTIVAL POPS CONCERT

❑   **6 – Indianapolis.** Victory Field. (800) 638-4296. Indianapolis Symphony Orchestra performance followed by spectacular fireworks. Concessions or bring your own picnic and blanket. Free. (Night before race)

INDIANAPOLIS 500 MILE RACE

❑   **6 – Indianapolis.** Motor Speedway. (800) 638-4296. The world's largest one-day sporting event. Admission. (Memorial Day)

FAMILY FUN FESTIVAL

3 – Cutler. Adams Mill. (765) 463-7893. Mill tours, old-fashioned games, hayrides, pony rides. No Admission. (Mid-month Sunday)

CHILDREN'S FESTIVAL

4 – Anderson. Citizen's Plaza. (765) 649-7215. Games, clowns, toys, kids crafts, face painting, food. No Admission. (Mid-month Sunday)

HARRISON COUNTY POPCORN FESTIVAL

8 – Corydon. Courthouse Square. (888) 738-2137. Celebrate the county's popcorn industry. Parade, popcorn demos and contests, popcorn-related foods. No Admission. (Mid-month weekend)

JUNE

STRAWBERRY FESTIVALS

Sample strawberry treats like fresh strawberry shortcakes and strawberry ice cream or sundaes. Entertainment. Kids activities.

- ❑   **1 – Wabash**. Historic Downtown. Very Berry Strawberry Fest. (219) 563-1420. No Admission. (2nd Saturday)
- ❑   **3 – Crawfordsville**. Historic Lane Place. (800) 866-3973. No Admission. (2nd weekend)
- ❑   **3 – Lafayette**. YWCA, 6th & Cincinnati Streets. (765) 742-0078. Admission. (1st Saturday)
- ❑   **7 – Jasper**. Lions Club, Riverview Park. (812) 482-4609. No Admission. (2nd Saturday)
- ❑   **9 – Madison**. On Broadway. (800) 559-2956. No Admission. (2nd Saturday)
- ❑   **9 – Metamora**. Along the canal. (812) 663-6600. No Admission. (1st weekend)
- ❑   **9 – Moores Hill**. Carnegie Hall. (812) 744-4015. No Admission. (2nd Saturday)

INDIAN POW WOWS

Authentic Native American music, dance, food- fry bread, buffalo, storytelling, arts, clothing, history and language.

- ❑   **4 – Anderson**. Adena-Hopewell Rendezvous. Mounds State Park. (800) 533-6569. Admission. (2nd weekend)
- ❑   **4 – Muncie**. Woodland Nations. Minnetrista Cultural Center. (765) 282-4848.
- ❑   **6 – Indianapolis**. Indian Market. Eiteljorg Museum. (317) 636-WEST. Admission. (Last weekend)
- ❑   **9 – Batesville**. Heritage Festival. (812) 934-4746. (1st weekend)

MARSHALL COUNTY HOT AIR AFFAIR BALLOON FESTIVAL

1 – **Plymouth**. Centennial Park. (219) 936-3311. Multiple ascension of hot air balloons at dawn and dusk. Food. No Admission. (2nd weekend)

EGG FESTIVAL

1 – **Mentone**. Menser Park. (219) 353-7417. The egg basket of the Midwest features the incredible edible egg in a parade, tractor pull, crafts, variety show. No Admission. (1st weekend)

COLE PORTER FESTIVAL

1 – **Peru**. Miami County Museum. (765) 473-9183. Cole Porter is celebrated as a native of this town with musical entertainment, memorabilia display, van tours. Admission. (2nd Saturday)

ROUND BARN FESTIVAL

1 – **Rochester**. Downtown, Main Street. (219) 224-2666. Round barn tours, bed races, rodeo, pet parade, kiddy races, wall rock climbing, food, entertainment, games. No Admission. (2nd weekend)

ETHNIC FESTIVAL

1 – **South Bend**. Howard Park & East Race Waterway. (219) 235-9952. Variety of ethnic foods and entertainment. Children's activities and rides. No Admission. (3rd weekend)

CITY OF LAKES BALLOONFEST

1 – **Warsaw**. Central Park, Winona Lake, and other locations. (800) 800-6090. Hot air balloons, evening balloon glow, sailboat regatta, concerts, fireworks, food. No Admission. (Last weekend)

GREEK FESTIVAL

2 – **Fort Wayne**. Headwaters Park. (219) 489-0774. Greek food, music, dancing and art. Admission. (Last weekend)

JUNE (cont.)

GERMANFEST

2 – Fort Wayne. Headwaters Park Festival Center. (800) 767-7752. German heritage celebrated with folk music, dancing, food, kindertag, sports, exhibitions. Admission. (3rd week)

FESTOONED FESTIVAL

3 – Lafayette. Tippecanoe County Historical Museum. (765) 742-6905. Self-guided tours of historic homes trimmed with patriotic decorations, children's parade, entertainment, food. No Admission. (Last Saturday)

STREET FESTIVAL

3 – Linden. Town Hall/Community Center. (765) 339-4525. Visit the Linden Depot Museum, carnival, food, entertainment. (3rd weekend)

VICTORIAN GASLIGHT FESTIVAL

4 – Anderson. Historic West 8th Street. (800) 533-6560. See the Victorian era re-created with period entertainment, home tours, old-fashioned games, tea time, food, and a wonderfully lit walking tour at night. No Admission. (2nd weekend)

GLASS FESTIVAL

4 – Greentown. Downtown. (765) 628-6206. This town's birthday features tours of the glass factory (see chocolate glass), re-enactors, historical displays, children's activities, food, music, historical play. No Admission. (Mid-month)

WILBUR WRIGHT FESTIVAL

4 – Hagerstown. Wilbur Wright Birthplace & Museum, CR 750 East. (765) 489-4735. Home tours, life-size replica of the Wright Flyer, Wright's model airplanes, food, music, games, sky divers. No Admission. (3rd weekend)

BILL MONROE MEMORIAL BEAN BLOSSOM BLUEGRASS FESTIVAL

6 – Bean Blossom. Bill & James Monroe Festival Park & Campground. (615) 868-3333. Longest running Bluegrass Festival in the country features the Bill Monroe Bluegrass Hall of Fame and Museum. Admission. (3rd weekend)

ITALIAN STREET FESTIVAL

6 – Indianapolis. Holy Rosary Church. (317) 636-4478. More than 25 Italian meats, pastas, salads, desserts. Church tours, entertainment. Admission. (2nd weekend)

MIDDLE EASTERN FESTIVAL

6 – Indianapolis. St. George Orthodox Church. (317) 547-9356. Authentic food, dancing, music, cultural displays, cooking demos, tours. Admission. (2nd weekend)

HELMATFEST

7 – Ferdinand. 18th Street Park. (812) 482-9115. Celebrate German heritage with food, games, entertainment. (3rd weekend)

OFFICIAL INDIANA PICKIN' & FIDDLIN' CONTEST

7 – Petersburg. Prides Creek Park. (812) 789-2518. State championships in fiddle, guitar, banjo, mandolin and harmonica. Old-time singing and bluegrass bands. Admission. (3rd weekend)

NATIONAL FLAG CELEBRATION

7 – Vincennes. Various locations. (812) 882-4960. Red Cross/USO Canteen recreates W.W.II theme with patriotic choir concert, parade. No Admission. (Mid-month)

June (cont.)

RED, WHITE, & BLUE FESTIVAL

8 – Crothersville. Community School Grounds. (812) 523-3247. A patriotic salute to Flag Day includes a parade, hot air balloon race, carnival, entertainment. No Admission. (2nd weekend)

RAILROAD DAYS FESTIVAL

9 – North Vernon. City parking lot. (812) 346-7377. Salute the steel ties of railroading. Model trains, railroad events. No Admission. (2nd weekend)

JULY

JULY 4TH CELEBRATIONS

Live entertainment, parade, carnival, food, fireworks.

- ❑ **1 – Bremen**. Firemen's Festival. Sunnyside Park. (219) 546-2105. No Admission. (Week of July 4th)
- ❑ **1 – Elkhart**. Sky Concert. (800) 377-3579.
- ❑ **3 – Delphi**. Canal Days. Wabash & Erie Canal Park. (219) 965-2262. No Admission. Period encampment.
- ❑ **4 – Fishers**. A Glorious Fourth. Conner Prairie. (317) 776-6000. Reading of the Declaration of Independence. Admission.
- ❑ **4 – Muncie**. Riverfest. Minnetrista Cultural Center. (765) 282-4848. Model sailboat regatta. Admission. Three days.
- ❑ **5 – Brazil**. Rotary Club Annual 4th of July Festival. Forest Park. (812) 448-3357. No Admission. (Week of July 4th)
- ❑ **5 – Rockville**. July 4th Ice Cream Social. Billie Creek Village. (765) 569-3430. Grand cake walk. Admission.

☐ **5 – Sullivan**. Celebration of Independence. County Park & Lake. (812) 268-4836. Lighted boat parade. Admission. Three days.

☐ **6 – Indianapolis**. Fourth Fest. Pan Am Plaza. (317) 633-6363. No Admission.

☐ **6 – Indianapolis**. Ice Cream Social. President Benjamin Harrison's Home. (317) 631-1898. Period costumed characters roam the grounds and talk to you. Admission.

☐ **7 – Evansville**. Freedom Festival. Downtown riverfront. (812) 464-9576. Admission. (Entire week of July 4th)

☐ **7 – Loogootee**, Independence Day Celebration. West Boggs Park. (812) 295-2482. Admission.

☐ **8 – Corydon**. Old Settlers Day. Old Capitol Square. (812) 738-4890. Pioneer demonstrations. No Admission.

☐ **9 – Aurora**. Firecracker Festival. Lesko Park & Water Street. (812) 926-2625. No Admission. Three days.

☐ **9 – Metamora**. Old Fashioned 4th of July. Main Street. (765) 642-2194. No Admission.

☐ **10 – Highland**. Ridge Road. (219) 924-3912. No Admission. Weeklong.

☐ **10 – LaPorte**. Jaycees' 4th of July Celebration. (219) 324-5392. Over 50 years with fly over of military jets. Admission. Weeklong.

☐ **10 – Whiting**. Lakefront and Park. (219) 924-3912. No Admission. Weeklong.

CIRCUS CITY FESTIVAL

1 – Peru. Circus City Festival Arena. (765) 472-3918. Best amateur youth performances include flying trapeze, highwire, bareback riding. Carnival downtown. Tour Hall of Fame, rides, food. Admission. (Mid-month, weeklong)

July (cont.)

SWISS DAYS

2 – Berne. Downtown. Yodeling, folk dancing, concerts, cheesemaking factory tours, Swiss food and famous apple dumplings. No Admission. (Last weekend)

INDIANA HIGHLAND GAMES

2 – Fort Wayne. Zollner Stadium. (800) 767-7752. Sheepherding, bagpipes, Scottish dancing and food, competitions. Admission. (Last Saturday)

KEKIONGA GATHERING OF THE PEOPLE

2 – Fort Wayne. Tahcumwah Community Center. (800) 767-7752. Large intertribal celebration of Native American culture through dance, music, food, crafts and storytelling. Admission. (Last weekend)

THREE RIVERS FESTIVAL

2 – Fort Wayne. Headwaters Park. (219) 747-5556. Children's Fest, McDonald's Parade, music, raft race, fireworks. Admission to some events. (Mid-month, weeklong)

HOT DOG FESTIVAL

3 – Frankfort. Courthouse Square. (765) 654-4081. Hot dogs with every topping imaginable! Puppy Park with children's activities. No Admission. (Last weekend)

IRON HORSE FESTIVAL

3 – Logansport. Downtown. (219) 722-IRON. Tour a railroad museum, train excursions, open cockpit plane rides. International food festival, parade. (No Admission)

WAAHPAAHSHIKI PEOPLES POW WOW

3 – West Lafayette. Tippecanoe Amphitheater Park. (765) 423-4617. Intertribal pow wow, arts, food. Features Great Lakes Drums with hundreds of dancers. Admission. (2nd weekend)

HAYNES-APPERSON FESTIVAL

4 – Kokomo. Downtown. (800) 456-1106. The town celebrates its automotive history with Haynes Museum tours, car shows, a parade, carnival, food, and talent contest. No Admission. (1st weekend)

ETHNIC/INTERNATIONAL FESTIVAL

4 – Marion. Matter Park Shelter. (765) 662-8325. Free passports to many countries with sights, sounds and tastes of many nationalities. (July 4th)

ALOHA INTERNATIONAL

4 – Winchester. Willard Elementary School. (765) 584-6845. Hawaiian steel guitar artists from 26 states and several foreign countries perform. Grand Luau feast. Admission. (2nd weekend)

SCOTTISH FESTIVAL

6 – Columbus. Mill Race Park. (800) 468-6564. Bagpipe bands, sheepdog trials, Highland dancing, athletic competitions and traditional foods. Admission. (3rd weekend)

CIRCLEFEST

6 – Indianapolis. Monument Circle. (317) 237-2222. 30 different bands, premier food, children's activities. Kickoff to Brickyard 400 Festival. Admission. (Last Saturday)

RIVERFEST

7 – Evansville. Riverside Drive. (812) 424-2986. Four stages of entertainment, food, carnival, children's activities. (Last weekend)

July (cont.)

STRASSENFEST

7 – Jasper. Downtown. (812) 482-6866. German heritage with music, food, talent show. No Admission. (Last weekend)

WATERMELON FESTIVAL

7 – Owensville. Downtown. (812) 768-6391. All you can eat plus other foods, parade and contests. No Admission. (Last weekend)

CATFISH FESTIVAL

7 – Shoals. Downtown. (812) 247-2828. Fishing contests, food, bands, sporting events. No Admission. (1st weekend)

LIMESTONE HERITAGE FESTIVAL

8 – Bedford. Brian Lane Way. (800) 798-0969. An important Indiana resource, Bedford stone was used to build the Empire State Building and the Pentagon. Quarry tours, parade, fireworks, sculpture exhibits and competition. No Admission. (July 4th)

PUERTO RICAN PARADE

10 – East Chicago. Block Stadium. (219) 398-5419. Ethnic food, music, salsa, merengue, parade & picnic. Admission. (3rd weekend)

GRECIAN FESTIVAL

10 – Merrillville. 8000 Madison Street. Greek dancing, food , pastries, carnival, gifts. No Admission. (2nd weekend)

GAELIC FEST

10 – Valparaiso. Sunset Hill Farm. (219) 465-3586. Irish and Scottish celebration. Dance, music, food and arts/crafts. Admission. (3rd Saturday)

PIEROGI FESTIVAL

10 – Whiting. Historic Downtown. (219) 659-0292. Slovak and Polish delicacies, music, dancing, parade. No Admission. (Last weekend)

AUGUST

INDIAN POW-WOWS

Authentic Native American music and dance. Food- fry bread and buffalo. Storytelling. Traditional arts, clothing, history and language.

- ❑ **2 – Berne**. Swiss Heritage Village. Woodland and Plains Indians culture.
- ❑ **3 – Lebanon**. American Indian Council. 4 H Grounds Community Bldg. (765) 482-3315. Admission. (3rd weekend)
- ❑ **8 – Derby**. Indiana Indian Movement. LDS Park. (2nd weekend)

AIRSHOW

1 – Goshen. Municipal Airport. (219) 295-3177. Features civilian, military, and historical aircraft with aerobatics and demos. Admission. (2nd weekend)

GENE STRATTON-PORTER CHAUTAUQUA DAYS

1 – Rome City. Sylvan Lake. (219) 854-3790. Tea party, Birthday party in Cabin, lake cruises, tours of GSP's (famous author and nature photographer) lovely home and property, food, entertainment. Admission. (Early half of month)

WESTERN DAYS

2 – Andrews. Downtown. (219) 786-3848. Dress for the Old West with pioneer games for kids, chuck wagon meals, Nashville entertainment, parade. No Admission. (2nd weekend)

August (cont.)

WILD WEST FEST

3 – Lafayette. Richie Plaza. (765) 742-2313. Relive the Old West. Cowboy shootouts, carriage rides, entertainment, food. Admission. (4th weekend)

GLASS FESTIVAL

4 – Elwood. Callaway Park. (765) 552-0180. Glass factory tours include: Prestige Art Glass, SR 13 (765) 552-0688; Spencers Lapidary (marbles), SR 37 & SR 13 (765) 552-0784; The House of Glass, SR 28 (765) 552-6841. Food, carnival, volksmarch, parade. (3rd weekend)

SUMMER HEAT

4 – Muncie. County Airport. (765) 284-2700. See 45 hot air balloons rise along with air shows, entertainment. Admission. (2nd weekend)

POPCORN FESTIVAL

4 – Van Buren. Downtown. (765) 934-4888. 25c popcorn, popcorn goodies, parade, entertainment, children's activities, cruise-in, line dancing. No Admission. (3rd weekend)

ANTIQUE TRAIN & CAR FESTIVAL

5 – Spencer. Downtown Square. (812) 829-6146. Steam train ride from Indy to Spencer with train robbery daily at 4pm. Admission. (4th weekend)

SWEET CORN FESTIVAL

7 – Oakland City. Wirth Park. (812) 749-4464. Parade, entertainment nightly, rides, kids' day (Sat), homestyle dinners, corn dipped in butter. No Admission. (2nd weekend)

WATERMELON FESTIVAL

7 – Vincennes. Patrick Henry Drive & Main Street. (812) 882-6440. Free watermelon, food sidewalk sales, sports competition, games pageants, historic site tours. No Admission. (4th weekend)

SCHWALZER FEST

8 – Tell City. Hall Park. (812) 547-2385. Swiss-German heritage with authentic food, entertainment nightly, rides and market. No Admission. (Early weekend)

POTATO FEST

10 – Medaryville. Downtown. (219) 843-3371. Spuds with every imaginable topping, curly fries, numerous potato creations. (Mid-month weekend)

RENAISSANCE TIMES FESTIVAL

10 – Valparaiso. Porter County Exposition Center. (219) 464-9621. Period actors, re-creation of life in the 1500s including jousting, hunting, sewing, kids' crafts, theatrical and musical performances. Admission. (3rd weekend)

SEPTEMBER

INDIAN POW-WOWS

Authentic Native American dance & music. Food- fry bread, buffalo. Storytelling. Traditional arts, clothing, language & history.

- ❑   **1 – Warsaw**. Land of Lakes, Gathering of the People. Kosciusko County Fairgrounds. (219) 267-5315. Admission. Last weekend.
- ❑   **3 – Attica**. Potawatomi Festival. Wabash riverfront. (765) 762-2245. 3rd weekend.

September (cont.)

- ❑ **4 – Tecumseh Lodge**. Tipton County 4H Fairgrounds. (765) 745-2858. Admission. Labor Day Weekend.
- ❑ **7 – Evansville**. Native American Days. Angel Mounds. (812) 853-3956. No Admission. 3rd week.

STORYTELLING FESTIVAL

1 – Bristol. Nationally known storytellers entertain with tales and folklore. (2nd weekend)

AUTOFEST

1 – Elkhart. S. Ray Miller Auto Museum. (888) 260-8566. Famous museum tours, open antique, classic, vintage car and truck shows. Admission. (2nd Sunday)

BLUEBERRY FESTIVAL

1 – Plymouth. Marshall County. Centennial Park. (888) 936-5020. Largest 3 day festival in Indiana with blueberry treats like milkshakes, pie and ice cream. Parade, circus, fireworks, fair food. No Admission. (Labor Day Weekend)

KID-O-RAMA

1 – Wabash. Honeywell Center. (800) 626-6345. Arts education, antique carousel, wagon rides, kids theater, entertainment and crafts. Admission. for concerts. (2nd Saturday)

PUMPKIN TRAINS

1 – Wakarusa. Old Railroad. (219) 862-2136. Take a mini train ride to the patch and pick a free pumpkin. Admission. (September / October)

AUBURN-CORD DUESENBERG FESTIVAL

2 – Auburn. (219) 925-3600. Classic car showcase. Parade of Classics, automotive museums. Admission. (Labor Day Weekend)

MARSHMALLOW FESTIVAL

2 – Ligonier. Main Street. (219) 894-4159. The country's center for marshmallow making. Bake-off, marshmallow putting contest, games, rides, entertainment, parade, factory tours. No Admission. (Labor Day Weekend)

LABOR DAY BREAKOUT

3 – Crawfordsville. Old Jail Museum. (765) 362-5222. See the only rotary jail built in Indiana (cells turn). Music, entertainment, children's events, free refreshments. No Admission. (Labor Day)

DAN PATCH DAYS

3 – Oxford. Rommel Park. (765) 385-2251. Rodeo, draft horse pull, Dan Patch memorabilia (famous pacer horse), parade, entertainment, bingo. Admission. (1st weekend after Labor Day)

GLOBAL FEST

3 – West Lafayette. Morton community Center. (765) 775-5110. Celebrate the city's many cultures with international foods, cultural displays, dance, music. No Admission. (Labor Day Weekend)

REMEMBERING JAMES DEAN FESTIVAL

4 – Fairmount. Main Street. (765) 948-4555. Tour Fairmount Historical Museum and James Dean Museum. Parade, look-alike contest, entertainment with 50's music, dance contest, all James Dean movies playing. No Admission. (Last weekend)

September (cont.)

LITTLE ITALY FESTIVAL

5 – Clinton. Water Street. (765) 832-8205. Italian music and authentic food. Spaghetti-eating contest, grape stomping. No Admission. (Labor Day Weekend)

ETHNIC FESTIVAL

5 – Terre Haute. Fairbanks Park. (812) 232-2727. Sample the world through ethnic displays, costumes, music, dance and foods. No Admission. (Last weekend)

OKTOBERFEST

5 – Terre Haute. German Oberlandler Club. National Guard Armory. Enjoy the "Gemuetlichkeit" (fun and fellowship) of the old world scenery and German song and dance, food. Admission. (2nd and 3rd weekends)

GREEK FESTIVAL

6 – Indianapolis. Holy Trinity Greek Orthodox Church. (317) 283-3816. Meridian-Kessler neighborhood with homemade food and dance. Admission. (Early in the month)

WENS SKYCONCERT

6 – Indianapolis. White River State Park. (317) 266-9700. Broadcast music synchronized to fireworks display. No Admission. (Labor Day)

WESTERN FESTIVAL

6 – Indianapolis. Eiteljorg Museum & White River Park grounds. (317) 636-WEST. Mountainmen demos, cowboy storytellers, trick ropers, chili & BBQ state championships. Admission. (3rd weekend)

STEAMBOAT DAYS

8 – Jeffersonville. Riverside Drive. (812) 288-9295. Howard Steamboat Museum (makers of fine boats) open for tours. Children's rides, food, entertainment, exhibits of importance of early inland waterways. No Admission. (Labor Day Weekend)

WATERMELON FESTIVAL

8 – Brownstown. Courthouse Square. (812) 358-2930. All you can eat of the juicy red melon plus other foods, live entertainment and parade. No Admission. (2nd weekend after Labor Day)

PUMPKIN FESTIVAL

8 – French Lick. Downtown. (812) 936-2405. Big Pumpkin Parade, carnival, food. No Admission. (Last week)

PERSIMMON FESTIVAL

8 – Mitchell. Main Street. (800) 580-1985. Persimmon pudding and other novelty persimmon dishes plus bake-off. Parade, carnival, entertainment. No Admission. (Last full week)

AVIATION AWARENESS DAYS

8 – Salem. Municipal Airport. (812) 755-4541. Hot air balloon race, parachutists, aircraft. Entertainment, breakfast and lunch served. No Admission. (Labor Day Weekend)

INDIAN LAKES BALLOONFEST

9 – Batesville. Indian Lakes Resort. (812) 934-4767. Hot air balloon race, tethered rides, "kids karnival", food, spectacular "Fire in the Sky" on Friday. Admission. (2nd weekend)

FALL FESTIVAL

9 – Canaan. Village Square. (812) 839-4770. Pony Express mail run, Indian papoose contest, Indian painting contest, food, parade, entertainment. No Admission. (2nd weekend)

September (cont.)

PUMPKIN SHOW

9 – Versailles. Courthouse Square. (812) 689-6188. Carnival, concessions, contest, entertainment, parade. Giant pumpkin weighing and pumpkin foods. No Admission. (Last weekend)

WIZARD OF OZ FESTIVAL

10 – Chesterton. Downtown. (219) 926-5513. Oz Fantasy Museum tours, look-alike contests, meet some of the actual MGM Munchkins. No Admission. (3rd weekend)

MEXICAN INDEPENDENCE CELEBRATION

10 – East Chicago. Block Stadium. (219) 391-8474. Northern IN goes south of the border with food, cultural/historical exhibits of the Mexican people. Admission. (2nd weekend)

STEAM & POWER SHOW

10 – Hesston. Steam Museum. (219) 872-7405. Rated Top 10 Festival. Steam train rides across 155 scenic acres. Also see restored steam power plant, sawmill, antique engines, tractors. Admission. (Labor Day Weekend)

PORK FEST

10 – Kouts. Downtown. (219) 766-2867. In honor of the town's largest industry you'll find a parade, entertainment, hog calling contest, guess a pig's weight and best of all pork chop dinners. No Admission. (3rd Saturday)

OKTOBERFEST

10 – Michigan City. Lakefront. (219) 872-3206. International food, artistry, entertainment like dancing and music, rides. Admission. (Labor Day Weekend)

BALLOONFEST

10 – Valparaiso. Porter county Fairgrounds. (219) 462-7684. Midwest balloons with launch and glows, food, souvenirs. No Admission. (2nd weekend)

POPCORN FESTIVAL

10 – Valparaiso. Downtown. (219) 464-8332. In honor of the late Orville Redenbacher and his origin from this town. Popcorn parade, hot air balloon show, children's play areas, food, live entertainment. No Admission. (1st Saturday after Labor Day)

SEPTEMBER / OCTOBER

HARVEST FESTIVALS

Horses plow fields, antique tractors, chuckwagon-style dinner, corn shredding, tractor pull, hayrides, corn shucking competition and straw baling.

- ❑ **2 – Huntington**. Tillage Days. Northern Huntington County. (219) 672-3331. No Admission. (2nd Saturday in September)
- ❑ **3 – Cutler**. Collage Festival. (765) 268-2635. No Admission. (Last Saturday in September)
- ❑ **4 – Fishers**. Agricultural Fair. Conner Prairie. (800) 966-1836. Admission. (Last weekend in September)
- ❑ **5 – Rockville**. Steam Harvest Days. Billie Creek Village. (765) 569-3430. Admission. (Labor Day Weekend)
- ❑ **6 – Geneva**. Limberlost State Historic Site. (219) 368-7518. No Admission. (1st Saturday in October)
- ❑ **7 – Bourbon**. Antique Engine & Tractor Show. (219) 342-0571. Admission. (Labor Day Weekend)
- ❑ **7 – Ferdinand**. SR 164. (812) 367-1206. No Admission. (3rd Saturday in October)

SEPTEMBER / OCTOBER (cont.)

- ❑ **7 – Vincennes**. Harvest Moon Homecoming.
  (812) 882-7422. (Last Saturday in October)
- ❑ **8 – Lanesville**. Heritage Weekend. Heritage Park. (812)
  952-2624. No Admission. (2nd weekend in September)
- ❑ **9 – Brook**ville. (765) 962-7415. Admission.
  (Last weekend in September)
- ❑ **10 – Wanatah**. Scarecrow Festival. US 421 & US 30.
  (219) 733-2183. No Admission. (Last weekend in
  September)

FALL PLAYLANDS

Corn Mazes, Hayrides, Petting Animals, Pick-a-Pumpkin patches,
Scarecrows, Painted Pumpkins, Pumpkin Carving Contests,
refreshments and entertainment.

- ❑ **1 – Goshen**. Kercher's Sunrise Orchards. CR 38.
  (219) 533-6311. (Mid-September to Mid-October)
- ❑ **1 - Legionier**. Pumpkin Fantasyland. 1680 Lincolnway
  West. (800) 254-8090. (October)
- ❑ **1 – Peru**. Tate Orchard / Apple Dumpling Inn.
  (765) 985-2467.
- ❑ **1 – Wakarusa**. Old Wakarusa Railroad. (219) 862-2714.
  Mini-train rides. (October)
- ❑ **2 – Bluffton**. Nostalgia Festival. Wells County 4-H
  Fairgrounds. (219) 622-6820. No Admission.
  (1st weekend in October)
- ❑ **2 – Bryant**. Scarecrow Contest. Bearcreek Farms. (800)
  288-7630. (1st half of October)
- ❑ **2 – Fort Wayne** Zoo The Great Zoo Halloween. (219)
  427-6800. Merry-not-Scary trick or treat. Evenings.
  (Mid-to-end of October)
- ❑ **4 – Cambridge City**. Dougherty Orchards. (765) 478-
  5198. Admission. (September)

- ❑ **4 – Cambridge City**. Hayes Arboretum. (765) 962-3745. Admission. (September weekend evenings)
- ❑ **4 – Fishers**. Conner Prairie. (800) 776-TOUR.
- ❑ **4 – Noblesville**. Stonycreek Farm. (317) 776-9427. SR 38 East. Admission on weekends. Daily. (Late September – October)
- ❑ **6 – Indianapolis**. Waterman's Farm Market. (317) 357-2989. (October)
- ❑ **8 – Starlight**. Joe Huber Family Farm & Restaurant. I – 64 East to Exit 119. (888) 41-VISIT.
- ❑ **9 – Lawrenceburg**. Perfect Autumn Festival. Perfect North Slopes Ski Area. (812) 537-3754. Chair lift rides. Admission. (2nd weekend in October)
- ❑ **10 – Hobart**. County Line Orchard. (219) 947-4477. (October)

APPLE FESTIVALS

Apple peeling and pie-eating contests, apple foods demos, apple foods-pies, donuts, cider, butter. Carnival.

- ❑ **1 - Nappanee**. (800) 517-9739. No Admission. (3rd weekend in September)
- ❑ **1 – Peru**. Tate Orchard. (765) 985-2467. Apples and dumplings.
- ❑ **2 – Bryant**. Bearcreek Farms. (800) 288-7630.
- ❑ **2 – Kendallville**. (219) 347-1064. (1st weekend in October)
- ❑ **4 – Cambridge City**. Dougherty Orchard. 1117 Dougherty Road off US 40. (765) 478-5198. Apple jellies, petting zoo, aviary. Daily. (July – December)
- ❑ **4 – Lapel**. Grabow's Orchard. SR 13 off I-69. (765) 534-3225. Raspberries too!
- ❑ **4 – Richmond**. (765) 855-2752. (Early October)
- ❑ **4 – Sheridan**. Stuckey Farm Market.

SEPTEMBER / OCTOBER (cont.)

- ❑ **4 – Spiceland**. Eatons Orchard.
- ❑ **5 – Bloomfield**. Courthouse Square. (812) 384-8995. No Admission. (1st weekend in October)
- ❑ **5 – Cory**. Community Center. (812) 448-8457. No Admission. (Last full weekend in September)
- ❑ **5 – Rockville**. Billie Creek Village. (765) 569-3430. Admission. (1st weekend in October)
- ❑ **5 – Spencer**. Downtown Square. (812) 829-3245. No Admission. (3rd weekend in September)
- ❑ **6 – Danville**. Beasley's Orchard. (317) 745-4876. No Admission. (1st weekend in October)
- ❑ **7 – Chrisney**. (812) 359-4789. (1st weekend in October)
- ❑ **8 – Starlight**. Stumler Orchard. (812) 923-3832. No Admission. (1st weekend in October)
- ❑ **9 – Batesville**. Liberty Park. (812) 933-6103. No Admission. (Last full weekend in September)
- ❑ **10 – Hobart**. County Line Orchard. (219) 947-4477. (3rd Saturday in September)

OKTOBERFEST

German music and dance, food, parade, carnival and hayrides.

- ❑ **3 – Crawfordsville**. Downtown. (765) 364-0820. Admission. (Last Saturday in September)
- ❑ **3 – Lafayette**. Richle Plaza. (765) 742-2313. Admission. (3rd Saturday in October)
- ❑ **6 – Indianapolis**. German Park. (317) 888-6940. Admission. (2 weekends in September)
- ❑ **7 – Huntingburg**. Herbstfest. City Park at First & Cherry Streets. (812) 683-5699. (1st weekend in October)

- ❑ **7 – New Harmony**. Kunstfest. (800) 231-2168. Petting zoo, wagon rides, general store. No Admission. (3rd weekend in September)
- ❑ **8 – Seymour**. Downtown. (812) 522-1414. No Admission. (1st weekend in October)
- ❑ **10 – Lowell**. Commercial Avenue. (219) 696-0231. No Admission. (1st weekend in October)
- ❑ **10 – Whiting**. Historic Downtown. (219) 659-0292. No Admission. (1st weekend in October)

OCTOBER

PARKE COUNTY COVERED BRIDGE FESTIVAL

5 – Ten days in the middle of October. County celebrates Indiana's historic past with 32 Historic Covered Bridges.

- ❑ **Rockville** – Headquarters. Sample cooking and crafts. Bus tours.
- ❑ **Billie Creek Village** – America's largest gathering of turn-of-the-century craftsmen. 3 bridges, entertainment, horse-pulled wagon rides, authentic foods and costumes. Admission. BLACK ROUTE.
- ❑ **Bridgeton** – 245-foot double-span covered bridge above the dam, waterfall near a working gristmill. Weaver, crafters, food. RED ROUTE.
- ❑ **Mansfield** – Historic Village, 1820's water-powered grist mill, 1867 covered bridge. BLACK ROUTE.
- ❑ **Mecca** – 2 historic schoolhouses, covered bridge, 1800's outdoor metal jail, old clay tile factory, crafts, foods, and dancing on the bridge. BROWN ROUTE & RED ROUTE.
- ❑ **Montezuma** – Historic river town and home of the Wabash-Erie Canal bed, Aztec trading post, hog roast, hayrides, trail rides.

OCTOBER (cont.)

❑ **Rosedale** – Potato fields, antique farm equipment. RED
   ROUTE.
❑ **Tangier** – 5 covered bridges, serve Tangier's famous
   "buried roast beef". BLUE & YELLOW ROUTE.

ADAMS MILL TREASURE HUNT

3 – Cutler. Adams Mill. (765) 463-7893. Learn about the area's
history as you drive on a scavenger hunt to look for clues.
Admission. (4th Saturday)

INDIAN TRAILS FESTIVAL

4 – Anderson. 5th & Main Streets. (812) 427-3550. Tribute to
Woodland, Delaware and Cherokee tribes. Canoe rides and walks
along the White River on the same trail Indians once followed.
Authentic demos, crafts and foods. No Admission. (2nd weekend
in October)

WOODLAND INDIANS POWWOW

4 – Fishers. Conner Prairie. (800) 966-1836. Authentic Native
American music and dance, food, storytelling, traditional arts and
clothing. (October weekend)

ETHNIC EXPO

6 – Columbus. Downtown. (800) 468-6564. Ethnic food, music,
dancing, exhibits, parade, fireworks. No Admission. (2nd weekend
in October)

RILEY FESTIVAL

6 – Greenfield. Downtown. (317) 462-2141. Commemorate
James Whitcomb Riley's birthday! Parades, entertainment,
pumpkin contest, food. No Admission. (First Thursday – Sunday
in October)

SCOT IN HARMONY

7 – **New Harmony**. North Street. (812) 682-4488. A family festival celebrating the town's links to Scotland. Music, dancing, entertainment. Admission. (1st Saturday in October)

KIDS' FALL FUNFEST

10 – **Chesterton**. Indiana Dunes State Park Nature Center. (219) 926-1390. Storytelling, puppet shows, crafts, other hands-on activities to learn about nature, music, food. No Admission. (3rd weekend)

NOVEMBER

ETHNIC FAIR

1 – **Goshen**. Goshen College Union & church buildings. (219) 535-7545. Ethnic diversity with exhibits, traditional songs, food, dance. 25 countries represented. Admission. (1st Saturday)

WINTER CELEBRATION

6 – **Bloomington**. John Waldron Arts Center. (812) 334-3100. Tree lighting ceremony, Santa, stories and art workshops. Admission/workshops only. (Saturday after Thanksgiving)

CELEBRATION OF LIGHTS

6 – **Indianapolis**. Monument Circle. (317) 237-2222. Lighting of the "World's Largest Christmas Tree" plus singing from the Indianapolis Children's Choir. No Admission. (Friday evening after Thanksgiving)

A COURTYARD CHRISTMAS

8 – **Scottsburg**. Scott County Courthouse Courtyard. (812) 752-4343. 700 plus luminaries glowing, carriage rides, food, entertainment, parade with Santa, children's games and carolers. No Admission. (Saturday after Thanksgiving)

FESTIVAL OF TREES

Beautifully decorated trees for sale to benefit charity. Gift shops. Entertainment. (End of November)

- ❑ **2 – Fort Wayne**. Embassy Theatre. (219) 424-4071. Admission.
- ❑ **3 – Lafayette**. (765) 423-6198. Admission.
- ❑ **4 – Anderson**. Paramount Theatre. (765) 642-1234. Admission.
- ❑ **4 - Richmond**. (800) 828-8414.

NOVEMBER / DECEMBER

WINTER WONDERLAND TRAIN

1 – Wakarusa. Old Wakarusa Railroad. (219) 862-2136. Diesel train (mini) ride through decorated trees, bridges, buildings and tunnels with holiday music throughout. 30 minute rides. Dress warmly. (Thanksgiving – 1st weekend in January)

FESTIVAL OF GINGERBREAD

2 – Fort Wayne. Old City Hall Historical Museum. (219) 426-2882. Creations of fantasy gingerbread houses on display. (Children's to Professional categories) Admission. (Thanksgiving through mid-December)

FESTIVAL OF LIGHTS

Lighted roadways or walkways. Entertainment. Carolers. Santa. Themed with characters and historical events. (Evenings beginning the weekend of Thanksgiving through December unless noted otherwise)

- ❑ **3 – Frankfort**. TPA Park. (765) 659-3422. Admission.
- ❑ **4 – Fishers**. Conner Prairie. (800) 866-1836. Walk-thru. Admission.

- ❑ **4 – Marion**. International Walkway of Lights, Riverwalk. (800) 662-9474. Gift shop. Daily. No Admission.
- ❑ **4 – Parker City**. Christmas Lights at ME's Zoo. (765) 468-8559.
- ❑ **5 – Brazil**. Christmas in the Park. Forest Park. (812) 448-8457. No Admission.
- ❑ **6 – Bloomington**. Winterfest Holiday Park. Monroe County Fairgrounds. 2 mile drive through.
- ❑ **6 – Columbus**. Mill Race Park. (800) 468-6564. Over 1.5 million lights. Admission.
- ❑ **6 – Indianapolis**. Christmas at the Zoo. Indianapolis Zoo. (317) 630-2001. 700,000 lights and 180 displays. Train & Trolley Rides. Admission.
- ❑ **6 – Indianapolis**. Winterland Holiday Light show. Indiana State Fairgrounds. (317) 927-7500. 5 million lights for 2.5 miles drive thru. Midwest's largest. Admission.
- ❑ **7 – Evansville**. Holiday Zoo Festival. Mesker Park Zoo. (812) 428-0715. Admission. 2 weeks before Christmas.
- ❑ **7 – Petersburg**. Christmas in the Park. Hornady Park. (812) 354-8155. Drive thru with over 1 million lights, 114 displays and live nativity scene. No Admission.
- ❑ **7 – Santa Claus**. (812) 937-2848. Tour thru Christmas Lake Village.
- ❑ **9 – Metamora**. Old Fashioned Christmas Walk. (765) 647-2109. Luminaries along roads and canal banks.
- ❑ **9 – Rising Sun**. Holiday Winter Walk. (888) RSNG SUN. Turn of the century light display on the riverfront. No Admission. Saturday only.
- ❑ **10 – Merrillville**. Hidden Lake Park. (219) 769-8180. 2 mile drive thru. Daily. Admission.
- ❑ **10 – Michigan City**. Washington Park. (800) 634-2650.

DECEMBER

HOLIDAY OPEN HOUSES

Holiday decorated historic homes with costumed interpreters and special music and refreshments.

- ☐ **1 – Bristol.** A Victorian Christmas Celebration. Elkhart County Museum. (800) 517-9737. (1st weekend)
- ☐ **1 – Elkhart.** Ruthmere Museum. (800) 517-9737. (1st Sunday)
- ☐ **1 – South Bend.** A Victorian Christmas. Copshaholm. (219) 235-9664. Admission. (Thanksgiving weekend to mid-December)
- ☐ **4 – Anderson.** Gruenewalt House. (317) 646-5771. (2nd Sunday before Christmas)
- ☐ **4 – Cambridge City.** Family Christmas Festival at Huddleston Farmhouse Inn. (765) 478-3172. (Early to mid-December)
- ☐ **4 – Kokomo.** Christmas at the Seiberling Mansion. (765) 452-4314. Admission. (Thanksgiving weekend to 3rd week of December)
- ☐ **4 – Richmond.** Christmas at Wayne County Museum. (765) 962-5756. (1st Sunday in December)
- ☐ **6 – Nashville.** T.C. Steele State Historic Site. (812) 988-2785. No Admission. (Mid-December)
- ☐ **7 – Gentryville.** Christmas through the Ages at Col. William Jones State Historic Site. (812) 937-2802. (Mid-December weekend)
- ☐ **7 – New Harmony.** (812) 682-4488. Admission. (1st Saturday)
- ☐ **9 – Madison.** Nights Before Christmas in Historic District. (812) 265-2956. Admission. (Thanksgiving weekend to 1st weekend in December)

- ❏   **9 – Vevay**. Over the River and Through the Woods, Downtown. (800) HELLO-VV. Admission. (1st weekend)
- ❏   **10 – LaPorte**. Poinsettia Festival. 7 acres of blooming poinsettias at Bernaacchi Greenhouse. (Last weekend of November)
- ❏   **10 – Lowell**. Christmas at Buckley Homestead. (219) 696-6769.
- ❏   **10 – Michigan City**. Christmas at Barker Mansion. (800) 634-2650. Admission. (1st Saturday in December to mid-January)
- ❏   **10 – Porter**. Christmas in the Dunes. Chellberg Farm & Bailly Homestead. (219) 926-7561. (2nd Sunday)

WINTERFEST

1 – Elkhart. Downtown. (800) 517-9737. Holiday parade, tree lighting, breakfast with Santa. (1st full week)

DOWNTOWN FOR THE HOLIDAYS

1 – South Bend. (219) 235-9952. Santa arrives, tree lighting ceremony, movies, Christmas tea, ice skating. No Admission. (2nd weekend)

LIVE NATIVITY SCENE

2 – Shipshewana. 210 N. Van Buren Street. (219) 768-4725. Costumed interpreters re-enact and celebrate the birth of Christ. Live animals and caroling too. No Admission. (3rd weekend in December)

DICKENS OF A CHRISTMAS

3 – Lafayette. Riehle Plaza. (765) 742-2313. Dickens' characters in a parade, holiday lighting ceremony, carriage rides. No Admission. (1st Saturday in December)

DECEMBER (Cont.)

ENCHANTED GARDENS LUMINARIA WALK

4 – Muncie. Oakhurst Gardens. (765) 741-5113. Sparkling lights along the path. Children's activities, refreshments, musicians and caroling. Admission. (2nd weekend)

JINGLE BELL JOURNEY & SANTA'S SHOPPE

4 – Muncie. YWCA. (765) 284-3345. Storyteller guides kids through a story acted out as they pass by displays. Santa's shop with inexpensive gifts and elves to help. (First three Saturdays in December)

PARKE COUNTY COVERED BRIDGE CHRISTMAS

5 – Rockville. Parke County Fairgrounds & other locations. (765) 569-5226. Travel through historic covered bridges and villages decorated for the holidays. Shopping, food. No Admission. (1st weekend)

CHRISTMAS IN THE PARK CONTEST

5 – Terre Haute. Deming Park. (812) 232-2727. Non-profit groups decorate city park shelters. Judged. Holiday train rides. No Admission. (Month-long)

CHRISTMAS WALK

5 – Terre Haute. Fowler Park Pioneer Log Village. (812) 462-3391. Historic village streets decorated for the holidays, dulcimer music, refreshments. Dress warmly, bring a flashlight. No Admission. (1st weekend)

SANTA CLAUS POST OFFICE

7 – Santa Claus. Hwy 162 and 245. (812) 937-4469. Nation's only post office with a "Santa Claus" postmark. (Daily except Sunday)

WINTERFEST

9 – Lawrenceburg. Perfect North Slopes Ski Area. (812) 537-3754. Ice sculpture demos, children's games on the snow, entertainment and carriage rides. Admission. (1st weekend in December)

SLEDDING AND TUBING ON THE DUNES

10 – Porter. Indiana Dunes State Park. (219) 926-1952.

LIVE NATIVITY

10 – Valparaiso. Courthouse. Live Nativity with animals. Caroling, carriage rides, refreshments, pictures with Santa. No Admission. (2nd Saturday)

HOME FOR THE HOLIDAYS

10 – Whiting. Downtown Community Center & surrounding area. Traditional ethnic customs, teddy bear tea, lighted parade. Admission to some events. (1st weekend)

NEW YEAR'S EVE CELEBRATION

Non-alcoholic party includes music, dance, clowns, storytellers, magicians, juggling and fireworks.

- ❑ **1 – Elkhart.** FamilyFest. (800) 262-8161. Admission.
- ❑ **7 – Evansville.** First Night. (812) 422-2111. Admission.

Chapter 3

INDIANA HISTORY & GOVERNMENT

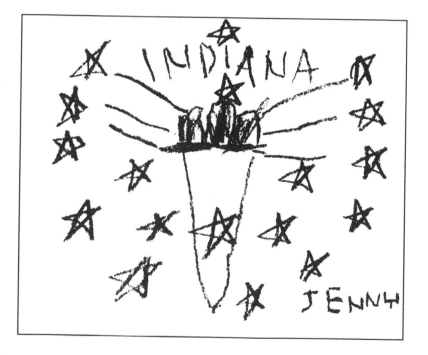

ELKHART COUNTY MUSEUM
SR 120. Rush Memorial Center, **Bristol**

- ❑ **Area: 1**
- ❑ Telephone Number: (219) 848-4322
- ❑ Hours: Wednesday - Friday, 10:00 am - 4:00 pm
  Sunday, 1 - 5:00 pm
- ❑ Admission: Donations accepted
- ❑ Miscellaneous: 13 rooms include a Victorian row house, a
  one-room school, a train depot, a general store, a dentist, a
  barber, a pharmacy and a tool room. See one of the earliest
  toy trains made of cast iron.

GRISSOM AIR MUSEUM
US 31 (6500 Hoosier Boulevard next to Grissom Air Reserve Base), **Peru**

- ❑ **Area: 1**
- ❑ Telephone Number: (765) 688-2654
- ❑ Hours: Tuesday - Saturday, 10:00 am - 4:00 pm. Closed
  January and Holidays.
- ❑ Admission: Free
- ❑ Miscellaneous: Theater. Gift Shop.

Outdoor display includes B-17 Flying Fortress, the sleek, fast B-58 Hustler and the fighter A-10 Warthog - plus 12 more planes. The Museum is set in a cockpit of a Phantom jet. View a flight trainer, displays of uniforms, models, survival gear (very interesting), and plane instruments.

MIAMI COUNTY MUSEUM
51 North Broadway (Downtown, US 24 and US 31), **Peru**

- ❑ **Area: 1**

- ❑ Telephone Number: (317) 473-9183
- ❑ Hours: Tuesday - Saturday, 10:00 am - 5:00 pm
- ❑ Admission: General $1.00
- ❑ Tours: By appointment
- ❑ Miscellaneous: Miami Indians, trading posts, circuses, Cole Porter (composer and song writer) hometown tribute with display of Grammy and 1955 Fleetwood Cadillac. Drug store, dentist office, penny scales, and quarter player piano.

FULTON COUNTY MUSEUM AND VILLAGE

Tippecanoe River and US 31 North
Rochester

- ❑ **Area: 1**
- ❑ Telephone Number: (219) 223-4436
- ❑ Hours: Monday - Saturday, 9:00 am - 5:00 pm
- ❑ Admission: Free
- ❑ Miscellaneous: Gift Shop. Indian and American apparel and toys.

This county is the "Round Barn Capitol of the World" and a central part of your visit is a restored 1924 round barn museum with farm machinery and tools. The museum also features themed rooms like Homes, Toys, Hospitals, Indians, Transportation, General Stores, Schools and Sports, Military, Recreation, Business, Churches, and the Circus. Each room gives you information on little known facts. Another extra touch is the Living History Village called "Loyal, Indiana" where you walk from the depot to a jail, log cabin, blacksmith shop, stagecoach inn, print shop and windmill. The village is only open on Saturdays and during Festivals.

NORTHERN INDIANA CENTER FOR HISTORY

808 West Washington Street, **South Bend**

- ❑ **Area: 1**
- ❑ Telephone Number: (219) 235-9664
- ❑ Hours: Tuesday - Saturday, 10:00 am - 5:00 pm
  Sunday, Noon - 5:00 pm. Groups by appointment
- ❑ Admission: Adults, $ 2.50 - $6.00, Children, $2 - $4.00
  depending on activity
- ❑ Tours: of Copshaholm, founders of Oliver Chilled Plow
  Works on premises.
- ❑ Miscellaneous: Gift Shop - mostly decorative items.
  Memberships available.

History Center - Pick up phones, push buttons or play a circular table board game of Agronomy (GO BACK, GO TO..., MOVE___SPACES). Other highlights were the All American Girls Baseball League displaying uniforms of the South Bend Blue Sox along with actual photos of team members. The "girls" were coached to be extremely feminine while playing the game. See examples of major manufacturing companies in the area (ex. honey, mint production).

Kids First Children's Museum - The large open room takes children on a trip along St. Joseph's River. From Native American dwellings (good picture opportunities of kids sitting in a canoe dressing in costumes, trading furs, tracking animals or relaxing in a wig-wam)...to agriculture (become a worm and slide on a dirt hill), to the industrial boom. Here you pretend you're an assembly line worker building a car that has to be inspected at the end of the line. Very creative and pretend fun!

WABASH COUNTY MUSEUM
South Wabash Street, **Wabash**

- **Area: 1**
- Telephone Number: (800) 563-1169
- Hours: Tuesday - Saturday, 9:00 am - 2:00 pm.
  (Summers and Winters until 1:00 pm)
- Admission: Free
- Miscellaneous: Civil War. Indians. Hometown of Crystal Gayle. Fossils. Costume doll collection.

KOSCIUSKO COUNTY JAIL MUSEUM
Winona Lake

- **Area: 1**
- Telephone Number: (219) 269-1078
- Hours: Thursday - Saturday, 10:00 am - 4:00 pm
  Sunday, 1 - 4:00 pm
- Admission: Donation
- Miscellaneous: The white stone building served as a public jail from 1871-1982. Nostalgic items are displayed in renovated jail cells and sheriff's living quarters.

SWISS HERITAGE VILLAGE
1200 Swiss Way (off 500 South and SR 27. Follow signs), **Berne**

- **Area: 2**
- Telephone Number: (219) 589-8007
- Hours: Monday - Saturday, 10:00 am - 4:00 pm
  (May – October)

❑   Admission: Adults $3.50, Students $1.00
❑   Miscellaneous: Swiss Way Cheese Company next door
     gives pre-arranged tours weekdays (best between 10:00 am
     - Noon). (219) 889-3531. Try their flavored cheeses (like
     garlic and onion!).

A s you enter the town of Berne, you instantly know it. Almost
    all of the buildings in town on SR 27 have a "Swiss look" to
their store fronts. The village has eight historic buildings moved to
one site. The Mill has the world's largest cider press. This, and
other interesting facts are presented as you take the living history
tours.

ADAMS COUNTY MUSEUM
420 West Monroe Street, **Decatur**

❑   **Area: 2**
❑   Telephone Number: (219) 724-2341
❑   Hours: Sunday, 1 - 4:00 pm (June – September)
❑   Admission: Donation
❑   Miscellaneous: Civil War, furniture, pioneer tools.

THE LINCOLN MUSEUM
200 East Berry (I-69 to SR 14), **Fort Wayne**

❑   **Area: 2**
❑   Telephone Number: (219) 455-3864
❑   Hours: Monday - Saturday, 10:00 am - 5:00 pm
     Sunday, 1 - 5:00 pm
❑   Admission: Adults $3.00, Seniors $2.00
     Children $2.00 (5–12)
❑   Tours: 12 +, $2.00/person
❑   Miscellaneous: Theaters and Museum Shops

The world's largest privately owned Lincoln collection is based on the theme (in the words of Lincoln), "Most governments have been based, practically, on the denial of equal rights of men. Ours began, by affirming those rights." A wonderfully presented museum, it takes you through the political life of Lincoln and his family. The first thing we were struck by were the numerous pictures / paintings of Lincoln without a beard--can you imagine? Interactive exhibits included the War Department telegraph room (plan Civil War strategies - what would you do?), a touch screen that lets you pretend you're Mr. and Mrs. Lincoln reading mail or modern day Lincoln Logs (1000's of them) to play with. Favorites are also the display of Lincoln's favorite songs, cake and friends or the "Dear Mr. Lincoln" desk where kids write letters to the President.

OLD CITY HALL HISTORICAL MUSEUM

302 East Berry Street (Downtown), **Fort Wayne**

- ❑ **Area: 2**
- ❑ Telephone Number: (219) 426-2882
- ❑ Hours: Tuesday - Friday, 9:00 am - 5:00 pm.
  Saturday - Sunday, Noon - 5:00 pm. (Closed January)
- ❑ Admission: Adults $2.00, Children $1.00 (6-18)

Explore the history of Allen County in the 100 year old sandstone city hall (looks like a castle). Favorites include the 1880's Street of Shops and the 1886 dollhouse. Go back further in time to the 1700's clash of Native Americans and early settlers (see Little Turtle's personal belongings and Anthony Wayne's camp bed). Before you leave, pretend to "do time" in the city jail or take a look at 1900's inventions created in Allen County or Indiana.

THE DAN QUAYLE CENTER AND MUSEUM

815 Warren Street. (I-69 at US 224 or US 24 exit. Downtown corner of Warren and Tipton Streets), **Huntington**

❑ **Area: 2**
❑ Telephone Number: (219) 356-6356
❑ Hours: Tuesday - Saturday, 10:00 am - 4:00 pm
    Sunday, 1 - 4:00 pm
❑ Miscellaneous: Large screen video presentation. Gift Shop.

America's only Vice-Presidential museum specifically dedicated to J. Danforth Quayle, 44th Vice-President. Trace Quayle's early years growing up in Huntington along with his political career. See his report card from local schools and pictures with Presidents. Exhibits and educational programs focus on the history and politics behind our nation's Vice Presidents with spotlights on the five Vice-Presidents from Indiana.

FORKS OF THE WABASH HISTORIC PARK

3010 West Park Drive (U524 and SR 9), **Huntington**

❑ **Area: 2**
❑ Telephone Number: (800) 848-4282
❑ Hours: Thursday - Sunday, 1 - 5:00 pm (May – October)
❑ Admission: Adults $2.00, Children $1.00 (12 and under)

After stopping in the Visitor's Center, start your visit of the museum and historical park that tells the story of the relationship between early European settlers and the Miami Indians (lots of trading) and the Miami and the US Government (treaties). The park includes a log schoolhouse, Nuck family pioneer house of German farmers and most interestingly, the home of Miami

Chief Richardville. The chief was considered a skilled negotiator in treaty talks and the wealthiest Native American in North America at his death.

HUNTINGTON COUNTY HISTORICAL MUSEUM
Court House (Top Floor, Downtown, SR 9 to US 24), **Huntington**

- ❑ **Area: 2**
- ❑ Telephone Number: (800) 848-4282
- ❑ Hours: Tuesday - Friday, 1 - 4:00 pm
- ❑ Admission: Donation
- ❑ Miscellaneous: Artifacts from Miami Indian Wabash and Erie Canal, Erie Railroad.

THE WINGS OF FREEDOM MUSEUM
1365 Warren Road, Huntington Municipal Airport, (I-69 to SR 5), **Huntington**

- ❑ **Area: 2**
- ❑ Telephone Number: (219) 356-1945
- ❑ Hours: Saturday, 10:00 am - 4:00 pm, Sunday, 1 - 5:00 pm
- ❑ Admission: Adults $4.00, Children (Free under 12)

The museum was created to preserve the legacy of pilots and their support crews who faced war to secure American freedoms. The central focus is a P-51D Mustang flown in successful combats by World War II fighter ace pilot, Brigadier General Robin Olds. There are also photos and artifacts tracing the history of military aviation.

TIPPECANOE BATTLEFIELD
909 South Street (SR 43 off I-65 Follow signs),
Battle Ground

- ❑ **Area: 3**
- ❑ Telephone Number: (765) 567-2147
- ❑ Hours: Daily, 10:00 am - 5:00 pm (March – November)
  Daily, 10:00 am - 4:00 pm (December – February)
- ❑ Admission: Adults $3.00, Seniors $2.00,
  Students $1.00 (age 5+)
- ❑ Miscellaneous: Interpretive Center museum and gift shop.
  Afternoon Adventure 3rd Saturday of each month - create
  1800's crafts, 2 - 4:00 pm. Approximately $20.00 per
  family. Also, monthly camp-ins, grades 4-6. Picnic/Shelter
  Grounds.

A significant spot where (because of the lack of unity between Tecumseh and The Prophet), the American Indian lost his final grip on the Midwest land he had roamed for thousands of years. Also, the same spot served for a rally in May, 1840 when over 30,000 people followed poor roads and trails to sing the praises of "Old Tipp" - General William Henry Harrison who had 28 years earlier bloodily claimed this battle ground for the Territory. The modern, festive political campaigns of today may have originated from the rally where roast beef, pork, stew and bread were served free. Catchy campaign songs capitalized the great presidency slogan, "Tippecanoe and Tyler, too!" as bands, speeches, floats and tales of the battle added flavor to the event. The museum has a fiberoptic map detailing moves of soldiers and Indians. 2 slide shows in theaters. The Battlefield has markers where officers died in battles.

TIPPECANOE COUNTY MUSEUM
909 South Street, **Lafayette**

- **Area: 3**
- Telephone Number: (800) 872-6648
- Hours: Tuesday - Sunday, 1 - 5:00 pm
- Admission: Adults $2.00, Children $1.50 (4+)
- Miscellaneous: Fowler House. Natural history, pioneers, Native Americans, Victorian era, railroads and industry.

CASS COUNTY MUSEUM
104 East Market Street, Jerolaman-Long House, **Logansport**

- **Area: 3**
- Telephone Number: (219) 753-3866
- Hours: Tuesday - Saturday, 1 – 5:00 pm
- Admission: Free
- Miscellaneous: Civil War. American Indian including prints by artist, George Winters. Log Cabin and Barn with period furnishings.

HISTORICAL MILITARY ARMOR MUSEUM
2330 North Crystal Street, **Anderson**

- **Area: 4**
- Telephone Number: (765) 649-TANK
- Hours: Tuesday - Saturday, 1 - 4:30 pm
- Admission: General $3.00, (age 6+)
- Tours: Reservation only
- Miscellaneous: Tank ride (reservation) $5.00/person, seasonally in good weather. (Riders must be at least 4 ft. tall)

W alk among fully operational and light armor vehicles dating from World War II to Desert Storm. Note President Harry S. Truman's 1947 official Cadillac limousine or the Howe Fire Truck. The building is labeled the "Mess Hall".

HUDDLESTON FARMHOUSE MUSEUM
838 National Road (US 40 West), **Cambridge City**

- ❑ **Area: 4**
- ❑ Telephone Number: (765) 478-3172
- ❑ Hours: Tuesday - Saturday, 10:00 am - 4:00 pm
  (Year round - except January)
  Sunday, 1 - 4:00 pm. (May – August Only)
- ❑ Admission: Free (Donation)

E xperience the life of an early pioneer farming family who opened their home to travelers for meals, provisions, shelter and feed/rest for horses. John and Susannah's home was built between 1839 and 1841 and includes a restored barn, three-story farmhouse, a springhouse and smokehouse. Many of the family's personal possessions like wooden bowls and special occasion parlor chairs, plus essentials for eleven children are displayed. Our favorite part of the tour was the basement where the Huddlestons apparently rented two "travelers' kitchens" used for cooking and sleeping.

CONNER PRAIRIE
13400 Allisonville Road, **Fishers**

- ❑ **Area: 4**
- ❑ Telephone Number: (800) 966-TOUR

❑ Hours: Tuesday - Saturday, 9:30 am - 5:00 pm, Sunday, 11:00 am - 5:00 pm (April – October)
Wednesday – Saturday, 9:30 am – 5:00 pm, Sunday, 11:00 am – 5:00 pm (November)
(Closed Christmas Day and New Year's Day Only)

❑ Admission: Adults $9.75, Seniors $8.75, Children $5.75 (5-12)

❑ Miscellaneous: 1823 William Conner House is a restored settler's and statesman's home - the finest in town. Tours every 20 minutes for $1.50 additional charge. Museum Center exhibits, gift shop and Prairietown Cafe (open for Lunch only).

Unlike many other historical villages in the Midwest, when you enter Prairietown, you really do interact as if you've been transported in time. All of the townspeople dress and act their character according to the year 1836. Mention of modern conveniences like pagers and cell phones is responded to with a blank stare. Your initial conversations may be a little awkward but you get the feel of things quickly. Pretend you're staying the night at the Golden Eagle Inn (for 12 ½ cents!) and then walk through town to visit neighbors like the Quaker printer, Jeremiah Hudson or the Fentons (weavers - you can purchase yarn dyed naturally) or the Campbells (Dr. and Mrs. - definitely upper class). The kids' favorites were the baby lambs just born in the Conner Barn and the Schoolhouse. Sit on split log benches as the school master gives you lessons teaching the "loud" school method where youngsters recite their different lessons aloud. Repetition is the key to learning and a ruler is used to discipline (not used on your first day of school, of course) . Allow enough time to spend with chores like candle dipping, washing clothes on a washboard, spinning, gardening or "not being underfoot" by playing with 19th century toys in the yard.

LEVI COFFIN HOUSE STATE HISTORIC HOUSE
US 27 (6 miles North of I-70 - Exit 151), **Fountain City**

❑   **Area: 4**
❑   Telephone Number: (765) 847-2432
❑   Hours: Tuesday - Saturday, 1 - 4:00 pm (June – August 31st). Saturday, 1 - 4:00 pm (September - October)
❑   Admission: Adults $2.00, Children $1.00 (6-18)
❑   Tours: Pre-scheduled school groups $0.50/person

O wned by the Coffins, this was an eight room refuge and rest home for slaves (up to 2000 total) on their escape North. The stop was part of the Underground Railroad so named because it was a secret stop between destinations. Some would stay a few days and others weeks until they felt well enough to travel on. You'll get to see the second floor hiding place. The owners, Levi and Catherine are characterized as Simeon and Rachael Halliday in the story "Uncle Tom's Cabin". This stop was so successful that all of the slaves who stopped here eventually reached freedom. What does the number of roses in a vase in the front window symbolize?

HOWARD COUNTY / SEIBERLING MANSION HISTORICAL MUSEUM
1200 West Sycamore (SR 22 off US 31), **Kokomo**

❑   **Area: 4**
❑   Telephone Number: (765) 452-4314
❑   Hours: Tuesday - Sunday, 1 - 4:00 pm. (Closed January)
❑   Admission: Adults $2.00
❑   Miscellaneous: The hand-carved woodwork and brass hardware of this elegant neo-Jacobean Romanesque

Revival mansion features the development of the county through memorabilia and antique car displays.

HENRY COUNTY HISTORICAL MUSEUM
606 South 14th Street, **New Castle**

- ❑ **Area: 4**
- ❑ Telephone Number: (765) 529-4028
- ❑ Hours: Monday - Saturday, 1 - 4:30 pm
- ❑ Admission: Free
- ❑ Miscellaneous: Former house owned by General William Grose, a commander during the Civil War. Clothing, musical instruments, tools.

HAMILTON COUNTY MUSEUM OF HISTORY
Noblesville Square, **Noblesville**

- ❑ **Area: 4**
- ❑ Telephone Number: (317) 770-0775
- ❑ Hours: Saturday, 10:00 - 2:00 pm
- ❑ Admission: Free
- ❑ Miscellaneous: 1875 museum that is the old Sheriff's residence and Jail houses more than 100 items.

WAYNE COUNTY HISTORICAL MUSEUM
1150 North "A" Street, **Richmond**

- ❑ **Area: 4**
- ❑ Telephone Number: (765) 962-5756

❑   Hours: Tuesday - Friday, 9:00 am - 4:00 pm,
     Saturday - Sunday, 1 - 4:00 pm
❑   Admission: Adults $3.00, Children $1.00 (+Group rates)

The Gaar family collections of Egyptian mummies (laid flat in a clear flat chest with push-button lighting for effect), Davis airplane, Richmond-made cars and Woolen desk. Outdoor Pioneer Village.

RANDOLPH COUNTY MUSEUM
416 South Meridian Street, **Winchester**

❑   **Area: 4**
❑   Telephone Number: (765) 584-1334
❑   Hours: Sundays, 2 - 4:00 pm (seasonally)
❑   Admission: Free
❑   Miscellaneous: 19th century brick home. Household
     utensils, tools, clothing, uniforms, and doctor's office.

CLAY COUNTY HISTORICAL SOCIETY MUSEUM
100 East National Avenue, **Brazil**

❑   **Area: 5**
❑   Telephone Number: (812) 448-8396
❑   Hours: Saturday - Sunday, 1:30 - 3:30 pm, (March -
     December)
❑   Admission: Free
❑   Tours: By appointment
❑   Miscellaneous: Old Post Office. Display of former
     resident, Orville Redenbacher, "Popcorn King".

BILLIE CREEK VILLAGE
US 36 East, **Rockville**

- ❑ **Area: 5**
- ❑ Telephone Number: (765) 569-3430
- ❑ Hours: Generally, 9:00 am - 5:00 pm. Adjust by season and festival. Call ahead.
- ❑ Admission: General $5.00, Seniors $4.50, Children, Free (age 4 and under)

A re-created 20th century village with 38 authentic buildings. As you enter the grounds, you'll pass through one of three covered bridges on the property (this area is well known for its covered bridges!). Stop in and visit a farmstead, a museum, a weaver, a potter, a jeweler or buy an old-fashioned treat or toy at the General Store. Demonstrations of the works of a candle-maker, broom-maker, and blacksmith occur throughout the day. Many people enjoy the mule-drawn wagon rides through the village and surrounding area.

HISTORICAL MUSEUM OF THE WABASH VALLEY
1411 South Sixth Street, **Terre Haute**

- ❑ **Area: 5**
- ❑ Telephone Number: (812) 235-9717
- ❑ Hours: Tuesday - Sunday, 1 - 4:00 pm, (February - December) . Craft demonstrations and history films on Sunday.
- ❑ Admission: Free
- ❑ Miscellaneous: Recreated General Store, post office, schoolroom, dressmaker's shop, bedroom, parlor, nursery, and toy shop.

PAUL DRESSER BIRTHPLACE
First Street and Dresser Drive, **Terre Haute**

❑ **Area: 5**
❑ Telephone Number: (812) 235-9717
❑ Hours: Sundays, 1 - 4:00 pm (Mid-May – September)
❑ Admission: Donation

Mr. Dresser wrote the famous, loved Hoosier song, "On The Banks of the Wabash". His birthplace home is that of the working class during pre-Civil War times with simple furnishings.

MONROE COUNTY HISTORICAL MUSEUM
202 East Sixth Street, **Bloomington**

❑ **Area: 6**
❑ Telephone Number: (812) 332-2517
❑ Hours: Tuesday - Saturday, 10:00 am - 4:00 pm
  Sundays, 1 - 4:00 pm
❑ Miscellaneous: Historic Carnegie Library.

CITY - COUNTY BUILDING
200 East Washington Street, **Indianapolis**

❑ **Area: 6**
❑ Telephone Number: (317) 236-4345
❑ Hours: Monday - Friday, 9:30 am - 5:30 pm
❑ Admission: Free
❑ Miscellaneous: Information card available.

28th floor observation tower (best if clear day, bring your own binoculars). City County Council meet the first and third Monday of each month at 7:00 pm (2nd floor Public Assembly room). 4th

graders and up (who are studying Indiana history) might be interested to see local government in action.

INDIANA STATE CAPITOL BUILDING
200 West Washington Street, **Indianapolis**

- ❑ **Area: 6**
- ❑ Telephone Number: (317) 232-9410 (when General Assembly is in session) . (317) 233-5293 (rest of year)
- ❑ Hours: Monday - Friday, 8:30 am - 4:30 pm
- ❑ Tours: Guided tours, 9:00 am - 3:00 pm
- ❑ Miscellaneous: Tour pamphlet at Information Desk for self-guided tour.

B uilt in 1882 on the site of the 1835 State House. Rotunda in the middle with North, South, East, West wings. See the Governor's office with state-seal rug. Even some door knobs are embossed with the state seal - nice touch. Also, his desk is made from teak decking from the USS Indiana. Sit in on General Assembly State Supreme Court when in session (older, quiet kids only) beginning in January. Supreme Court matters tend to be dealing with serious thought-provoking issues.

INDIANA WAR MEMORIAL
431 North Meridian Street, **Indianapolis**

- ❑ **Area: 6**
- ❑ Telephone Number: (317) 232-7615
- ❑ Hours: Daily, 8:30 am - 4:30 pm
- ❑ Miscellaneous: Self-guided tour using information cards at each display.

INDIANA STATE MUSEUM
202 North Alabama Street (Old City Hall, Downtown)
Indianapolis

- ❑ **Area: 6**
- ❑ Telephone Number: (317) 232-1637
- ❑ Hours: Monday - Saturday, 9:00 am - 4:45 pm
  Sunday, Noon - 4:45 pm
- ❑ Admission: Free
- ❑ Miscellaneous: Gift shop with many Indiana-made items

A 4-story Foucault pendulum is suspended from a stained-glass skylight in the rotunda. The main exhibits include:

- ❑ **When Nature Ruled**: early Indiana people and animals - geological past with dinosaurs and glaciers.
- ❑ **Streets of Indians**: living history variety store. Freetown Village black history depicting life of free black people after Civil War. Usually you can participate in dramas.
- ❑ **On The Air**: Indiana Radio and TV, 1920 - 1950 - hear and watch old stars like Red Skelton and Carole Lombard on the gallery's radios and televisions.
- ❑ **Sports**: Hold your hand up to one of a pro basketball player's - see movie clips from Indiana (theme movies like Hoosiers and Breaking Away). Uniforms from winning teams.

INDIANA SOLDIERS' AND SAILORS' MONUMENT
Monument Circle (Meridian Street, Center of Town... You can't miss it!), Indianapolis

- ❑ **Area: 6**
- ❑ Telephone Number: (317) 232-7615
- ❑ Hours: Daily, 11:00 am - 7:00 pm

❑   Admission: Free
❑   Tours: Observation deck open mid-April to mid-October

Challenge your energetic kids to the 336 stair climb to glass-enclosed balcony at the top for a panoramic view. (An elevator is available up to last 45 stairs). Bronze and limestone carvings (enormous and detailed) of famous Indianans like James Riley and President Harrison. The largest sculptures are of Civil Wartime Scenes. Throughout the years, its steps play to performers, politicians and festivals. Inside the base is a museum with interesting city and war insights. "Miss Indiana" tops the landmark with curved steps North and South and fountains with reflecting pools to the East and West.

PRESIDENT BENJAMIN HARRISON HOME
1230 North Delaware Street, **Indianapolis**

❑   **Area: 6**
❑   Telephone Number: (317) 631-1898
❑   Hours: Monday - Saturday, 10:00 am - 3:30 pm
      Sunday, 12:30 - 3:30 pm. (Hours vary in January)
❑   Admission: Adults $3.00, Seniors $2.50, Children $1.00
❑   Tours: Begin every 30 minutes, approximately 1 hour
❑   Miscellaneous: Gift Shop

See the 16 room Italianate Victorian home of the lawyer nominated for 23rd presidency in 1888. Stand on the front stoop where Benjamin Harrison gave 80 "front porch" speeches to 300,000 people who came by to listen. In the Master bedroom is displayed an old-fashioned home gym with weighted pulleys made from beautiful wood (a 19th century NordicTrack!) See the Library where election returns were tallied by telegraph. A piece of Haviland White House china that Caroline Harrison designed choosing corn to surround the border because it was "a crop indigenous to the North American Continent". See creations of the First Lady and artist, Caroline's paintings. Actual belongings of the Harrisons include inaugural Bible, White House Tea Set, Parlor Sofa – but don't touch!

BROWN COUNTY HISTORICAL MUSEUM

Museum Lane, Downtown, **Nashville**

- ❑ **Area: 6**
- ❑ Telephone Number: (812) 988-4153
- ❑ Hours: Weekends and Holidays, 1 - 5 :00 pm (May – October)
- ❑ Admission: Donations
- ❑ Miscellaneous: 1897 Doctor's Office, blacksmith, loom room, 1879 log jail (men were kept downstairs, women upstairs) and 1850's pioneer cabin.

ANGEL MOUNDS STATE HISTORIC SITE

8215 Pollack Avenue (I -164 to Highway 662, Covert Avenue Exit), **Evansville**

- ❑ **Area: 7**
- ❑ Telephone Number: (812) 853-3956
- ❑ Hours:, Tuesday - Saturday, 9:00 am - 5:00 pm, Sunday and Holidays, 1 – 5:00 pm (Mid-March – December)
- ❑ Admission: Donations
- ❑ Tours: By appointment (groups)
- ❑ Miscellaneous: Interpretive Center. Nature preserve. Picnic Area.

Located on the banks of the Ohio River, it's a preserved prehistoric Indian settlement of the Mississippians who planted corn, hunted and fished for food in the area for over 250 years. The Indians had 1000 - 3000 people populate the area. 11 earthen mounds served as elevated buildings until mysteriously abandoned. The site also includes reconstructed winter houses, a round house, summer houses and a temple that formed a village within the mounds. Learn about home and fortress construction - do you know what "waffle" and "daub" mean?-- (twigs woven between logs, then plastered with clay). The Middle-Mississippi tribe were known for their pottery and animal-shaped toys made from clay with added crushed mussel shells (used as a tempering agent) A popular kids game called "chunkey" is played by throwing spears at small rolling stone discs. The closest spear wins.

DUBOIS COUNTY COURTHOUSE
One Courthouse Square, **Jasper**

- **Area: 7**
- Telephone Number: (812) 481-7000
- Hours: Monday - Friday, 8:00 am - 4:00 pm
- Admission: Free
- Miscellaneous: 1911 Renaissance Revival style courthouse. Lobby display of local artifacts.

LINCOLN BOYHOOD NATIONAL MEMORIAL
SR 162 (2 miles East of Gentryville off I-64), **Lincoln City**

- **Area: 7**
- Telephone Number: (812) 937-4541
- Hours: Daily, 8:00 am - 5:00 pm

❑   Admission: General $2.00, Family $4.00
❑   Miscellaneous: Picnic Shelter.

Visitor Center is a museum with film "Here I Grew Up" (from age 7-21 years) - young Abe Lincoln. The Cabin site is a working pioneer farmstead with animals and crops where Abraham used to split rails, plant and plow or milk cows. See his mother's grave (she died of "milksick" when he was 9 years old). We learned that "milksick" is a disease caused by poisonous milk produced by cows that eat snakeroot (if pastures are dry, cows migrate to forest areas where poisonous plants grow). Walk on the Boyhood Nature Trails - the same trails that a young Abraham would have walked alone in thought years ago.

MARTIN COUNTY MUSEUM
North High Street, **Shoals**

❑   **Area: 7**
❑   Telephone Number: (812) 295-4093
❑   Hours: Sundays (every other) afternoons
❑   Admission: Free
❑   Miscellaneous: Infamous Archer Gang, pioneer artifacts.

GROUSELAND
3 West Scott Street (Downtown at Park and Scott Streets. Follow signs), **Vincennes**

❑   **Area: 7**
❑   Telephone Number: (812) 882-2096
❑   Hours: Daily, 9:00 am - 5:00 pm (except January, February, 11:00 am - 4:00 pm)
❑   Admission: Adults $3.00, Children $1 - $2.00 (under age 5 years)

❏   Tours: Ring the doorbell and a guide will escort you in.

The Home of William Henry Harrison, the 1ˢᵗ Governor of the Indiana Territory and later the 9ᵗʰ President of the United States. He died in office 31 days after his inauguration - some say unnecessarily due to blood letting. The dining room has a bullet hole in the window shutter where someone tried to shoot Harrison (they missed!). As you walk from upstairs down to the warming kitchen (do you know what a buttery is?), you'll see a cutaway of original flooring used in the home. The layers of clay and straw underneath wood provided insulation and noise protection (Harrison didn't want servants to eavesdrop). Stories for the kids include the "giant travel chest" and a Mother's apron needle used for more than sewing. Mr. Harrison is best known for his campaign against Tecumseh - The Treaty of Grouseland was signed at his home.

INDIANA MILITARY MUSEUM
43 Old Bruceville Road, **Vincennes**

❏   **Area: 7**
❏   Telephone Number: (812) 882-8668
❏   Hours: Daily, Noon - 4:00 pm. Winter hours vary.
❏   Admission: Adults $2.00, Students $1.00

Military history from the Civil War to Desert Storm. Outdoors - tanks, artillery, helicopters. Indoors - uniforms, flags, relics from battlefields, captured enemy souvenirs, World War II toys and homefront items.

INDIANA TERRITORY CAPITOL VILLAGE

1 West Harrison Street, Downtown, **Vincennes**

- ❑ **Area: 7**
- ❑ Telephone Number: (812) 882-7422
- ❑ Hours: Wednesday - Saturday, 9:00 am - 5:00 pm
  Sunday, 1 – 5:00 pm (Mid-March to Mid-December)
- ❑ Admission: Adults $2.00, Students $1.00
- ❑ Tours: Begin at Log Cabin Visitor's Center
- ❑ Miscellaneous: Videotape of Vincennes' history in the
  Visitor's Center.

S tart at the oldest major government building in the Midwest - the Indiana Territory Capitol Building. Then, stop in for a demonstration of old-fashioned printing presses at the Elias Stout Print Shop…a replica print shop where they first printed the Law of the Territory and the first Territory newspaper, "The Indiana Gazette". Learn where we got the phrase, "UPPER CASE or capital letters" and "mind your P's and Q's". Lastly, step inside Maurice Thompson's birthplace where the author of "Alice of Old Vincennes" (a best-selling romance novel) was born. It features frame construction instead of logs and a cast iron stove in place of a drafty fireplace - both modern for the time.

OLD FRENCH HOUSE AND INDIANA MUSEUM

First and Seminary Streets (US 50 / 41 By-pass to North
6th Exit to downtown), **Vincennes**

- ❑ **Area: 7**
- ❑ Telephone Number: (800) 886-6443
- ❑ Hours: Tuesday - Saturday, 9:00 am - Noon
  and 1 - 5:00 pm. Sunday, 1 - 5:00 pm (Summer)

❑ Admission: Adults $1.00, Students $0.50
❑ Miscellaneous: Exhibits trace four periods of American pre-history from the bones of a mastodon to the furnishings of the family life of a fur trader and Indian interpreter. Creole style home.

DAVIESS COUNTY MUSEUM
Old Jefferson School (CR 150 South. Off SR 57), Washington

❑ **Area: 7**
❑ Telephone Number: (812) 254-5122
❑ Hours: Tuesday - Saturday, 11:00 am - 3:00 pm. (October – April). Tuesday - Saturday, 11:00 am - 4:00 pm (May – September)
❑ Admission: $1.50 (12 +)
❑ Miscellaneous: Schools in area. Victorian furnishings and dolls, old license plates, church room, railroad room, medical room (early x-ray machine), military room, beauty/barber chair.

FLOYD COUNTY MUSEUM
201 East Spring Street, New Albany

❑ **Area: 8**
❑ Telephone Number: (812) 944-7336
❑ Hours: Tuesday – Saturday, 10:00 am - 5:30 pm
❑ Admission: Free
❑ Miscellaneous: Art and history. "The Yenawire Exhibit" - a hand-carved animated diorama depicting scenes from early Indiana.

JOHN HAY CENTER
307 East Market Street, Salem

- ❑ **Area: 8**
- ❑ Telephone Number: (812) 883-6495
- ❑ Hours: Tuesday - Saturday, 1 - 5:00 pm
- ❑ Admission. $2.00 (12+)

A reconstructed pioneer village with blacksmith, carriage house, jail, general store, school, church, and loom house. Hays' birthplace with 1840's furnishings and Stevens Memorial Museum – 19th century professional offices replicas are also part of the complex.

UNION COUNTY MUSEUM
East Railroad Street, Liberty

- ❑ **Area: 9**
- ❑ Telephone Number: (765) 458-5434
- ❑ Hours: Saturday, Sunday, and Holidays, 2 - 4:00 pm (June – August)
- ❑ Admission: Free
- ❑ Miscellaneous: Restored CSX Train Depot with stained glass windows. Local relics. Railroad memorabilia.

JEFFERSON COUNTY MUSEUM AND RAILROAD STATION DEPOT
615 West First and Mill Streets on Ohio River, Madison

- ❑ **Area: 9**
- ❑ Telephone Number: (812) 265-2335
- ❑ Hours: Monday - Saturday, 10:00 am - 4:30 pm, Sunday, 1 - 4:00 pm. (May – October) Weekdays only. (November – April)

- ❑ Admission: General $3.00
- ❑ Miscellaneous: Civil War, Steam boating, Store House, Victorian Parlor, Octagonal Railroad Station. Stop over to Dr. William Hutchings' Office (on West 3rd) or The Sullivan House (on West 2nd) for more historical county insight.

WHITEWATER CANAL STATE HISTORIC SITE
US 52 (8 miles West of Brookville), **Metamora**

- ❑ **Area: 9**
- ❑ Telephone Number: (765) 647-6512 or (765) 647-2109
- ❑ Hours: Tuesday - Saturday, 9:00 am - 5:00 pm. Sunday, 1 - 5:00 pm. (Mid March - Mid December)
- ❑ Admission: Free
- ❑ Tours: 30 Minute Canal boat tour, $1.00 /person. (May - October)
- ❑ Miscellaneous: Gristmill on site grinds grain for purchase. Old - fashioned entertainment.

Originally a town built around the canal between 1836-1847. The canal rides go through an 80 ft. covered wooden aqueduct lifting the canal waters 16 ft. above the creek. Also pass by a restored lock and by a gristmill. Hundreds of cute little shops (they made the stores very small, scaled down, mini-village look). Some "must stops" for kids are: Rattlesnake Pete's - for gem mining and viewing strange pets or Taste of Elvis - for ice cream. This is a full day excursion - if you don't mind crowds, we especially love all the extra activity and entertainment during festival weekends.

OHIO COUNTY HISTORICAL MUSEUM
212 South Walnut Street, **Rising Sun**

❑ **Area: 9**
❑ Telephone Number: (888) 776-4786
❑ Hours: Weekends, 1 - 4:00 pm (May-October)
❑ Admission: Free
❑ Miscellaneous: Home of "Hoosier Boy" a 1900 racing boat with fastest time between Louisville and Cincinnati. Auto Harp - first coin operated music player.

RUSH COUNTY MUSEUM
North Perkins and East 7th Streets, **Rushville**

❑ **Area: 9**
❑ Telephone Number: (765) 932-2880
❑ Hours: Sundays, 2 - 4:00 pm (Summer)
❑ Admission: Donation
❑ Miscellaneous: Over 1500 items

SWITZERLAND COUNTY HISTORICAL MUSEUM
Downtown, **Vevay**

❑ **Area: 9**
❑ Telephone Number: (812) 427-3560
❑ Hours: Daily, Noon - 4:00 pm (May - October)
❑ Admission: $1.00 (age 14+)
❑ Tours: By appointment
❑ Miscellaneous: Old 1860 Church houses museum.

JENNINGS COUNTY MUSEUM
North American House, **Vernon**

- **Area: 9**
- Telephone Number: (800) 928-3667
- Hours: Monday - Friday, 9:00 am - 4:00 pm
- Admission: Donation
- Miscellaneous: Elevated railroad, Underground Railroad, Morgan's Raid.

LAKE COUNTY MUSEUM
5800 Broadway (Old Lake County Court House), **Crown Point**

- **Area: 10**
- Telephone Number: (800) ALL-LAKE or (219) 663-0660
- Hours: Monday - Friday, 10:00 am - 5:00 pm.
  Saturday, 10:00 am - 7:00 pm
- Admission: Free
- Miscellaneous: 1878 Courthouse with central clock tower, Trial of John Dillinger, Cobe Cup Race.

LAPORTE COUNTY MUSEUM
State and Michigan Avenue, **LaPorte**

- **Area: 10**
- Telephone Number: (219) 326-6808
- Hours: Monday - Friday, 10:00 am - 4:30 pm
  1st Sunday, 1 - 4:00 pm
- Admission: Free
- Miscellaneous: 80,000 items. Family heirlooms. W.A. Jones' famous collection of antique firearms and weapons.

THE GREAT LAKES MUSEUM OF MILITARY HISTORY
1710 East US 20, **Michigan City**

- **Area: 10**
- Telephone Number: (219) 872-2702
- Hours: Tuesday - Friday, 9:00 am - 4:00 pm. Saturday, 10:00 am - 4:00 pm. Sunday (Summer), Noon - 3:00 pm
- Admission: Free
- Miscellaneous: Displays of memorabilia from all eras includes photos, weapons, medals, uniforms, World War II Declarations of War, and a 1905 Cannon. The first submarine was launched from these shores.

Chapter 4

THEME
RESTAURANTS

Toby Starr

DINERS / DRIVE-INS (CLASSIC 1950's)

❑   Area: Statewide
❑   Miscellaneous: Diners-50's motif. Burgers, malts and
    floats. Cruise-ins.

SCHOOPS

1 - Plymouth. 1410 N. Michigan. Off US 30. (219) 936-9970.
Lunch/Dinner.

MR. HAPPY BURGER

1 – Wabash. 3131 East Market. (219) 753-6418. Lunch/Dinner.
Carousel-look front, trolley car seats. Chicken, pizza, burgers.

YESTERDAY'S DINER

4 – Marion. 3015 South Washington St. (765) 664-CAFE.
Breakfast/Lunch. Order the King of Earl or Duke sandwich.

CLASSIC 1950'S DINER

5 – Rockville. Hwy. 41 & Parkway Dr. (765) 569-1950.

BILL'S FABULOUS 50'S

6 – Indianapolis. 6310 Rockville Rd. (317) 244-1950. Roller-
skating, Carhops, Outdoor Jukebox, Rootbeers & Coneys.

EDWARD'S DRIVE-IN

6 – Indianapolis. 2126 Sherman Drive (317) 786-1638. Carhops
specializing in frosty mugs of rootbeer and coney dogs.

NORTHSIDE DINER

10 – Porter. 100 N. Calumet Road, Downtown. (219) 926-9040.
Breakfast/Lunch. Since 1934. Homemade pies.

OLD FASHIONED SODA FOUNTAIN / PHARMACY

- ❑ Area: Statewide
- ❑ Miscellaneous: Coca-Cola collectibles. Old-fashioned sodas, shakes, malts. Long marble counters (easier to slide those phosphates down the row!) Penny candy. Original tin ceilings.

HOSTETLER'S MAIN STREET SHOPPE

2 - Shipshewana. (219) 768-4882.

REMINISCE-A-BIT

4 - Farmland. 101 N. Main Street. (765) 468-8934. Monday - Saturday, 10:00 am - 8:00 pm.

MALOTTCHI BROTHERS GRANDE SODA FOUNTAIN

4 - Greentown. 100 W. Main Street. (765) 628-9914. Daily, 11:00 am - 9:00 pm. (Friday, Saturday 10:00 pm).

ZAHARAKO'S

6 - Columbus. 329 Washington Street. (812) 379-9329. German pipe organ. Green river phosphate. "Zaharaoplastion" is Greek for Confectionery.

HOOKS

6 - Indianapolis. See Museums Chapter.

SCHMIFF'S CONFECTIONERY

8 - Jeffersonville. 347 Spring Street. (812) 283-8367. Famous for its cinnamon red hots.

DAS DUTCHMAN ESSENHAUS
240 US 20 (1 mile West of SR 13), Middlebury

☐ **Area: 1**
☐ Telephone Number: (219) 825-9471
☐ Hours: Daily, 6:00 am – 8:00 pm (except Sunday)
☐ Miscellaneous: Amish Country Decor restaurant complex includes a bakery, candymakers, and Amish crafts. Buggy rides along carriage trails and through a covered bridge are available while you wait for your table.

OLD WAKARUSA RAILROAD COME AND DINE RESTAURANT
SR 19. (Indiana Toll Road to SR 19 South - 13 miles). Wakarusa

☐ **Area: 1**
☐ Telephone Number: (219) 862-2714)
☐ Hours: Daily, except Sunday, 11:00 am - Dark (Railroad, April – October)
☐ Miscellaneous: Come and Dine Restaurant - Amish Country Cooking. 6:00 am - 9:00 pm. Bakery and gift shop. Antique tractor display.

A one and one-half mile ride on a 1/3 replica of the famous General Locomotive past a "mini-village". You'll start by going under an overpass, then past a miniature water tower, over low hills, past a small lake, through a long tunnel and even intersect one stretch of a local street. With everything miniature, it's just the right size for your little ones and s-o-o-o cute to watch and ride! Our kids each got an engineer's cap (pink for girls and blue for boys) which added to the excitement.

OLD #3 FIREHOUSE CAFE AND MUSEUM

226 West Washington Boulevard, **Fort Wayne**

- ☐ **Area: 2**
- ☐ Telephone Number: (219) 426-0051
- ☐ Hours: Monday - Friday, 11:00 am – 2:00 pm
- ☐ Miscellaneous: Just above the Firefighter's Museum is a Cafe where you are surrounded by antique fire engines and firemen's uniforms and tools. Try a "Life Net" or "Hook and Ladder" sandwich all set in Fort Wayne's old Engine House #3 building. Say "Hi" to all the Dalmatian for us.

THE HOME OF ELIAS RUFF RESTAURANT

Main Street (Behind Antiques Shopping Complex), **Grabill**

- ☐ **Area: 2**
- ☐ Telephone Number: (219) 627-6312
- ☐ Hours: Daily, 11:00 am - 8:00 pm

Pretend you're a traveling pioneer family for a day and stop at the 200 year old reconstructed roadhouse. All furnishings are period 1800's including the "pie safe", the oil lamps at each table, and the large cupboard that opens up to serve from the kitchen. While it is suggested one-person order the Blue Plate Special (old country recipes served on a speckled blue tin plate) another must order the Moo-oink Sandwich. It's the house sandwich handed down from family to family since 1850 and is a ground beef burger with added special ingredients (can you guess one oink-oink?). Our vote for the best burger ever!

PIZZA JUNCTION
201 Court Street, **Huntington**

❑ **Area: 2**
❑ Telephone Number: (219) 356-4700
❑ Hours: Sunday - Thursday, 11:00 am - 11:00 pm
   Friday - Saturday, 11:00 am - 1:00 am

L ocated by the railroad tracks in a restored train depot. Hopefully, several trains will go past. Actual restored photos of historic buildings around town (like Nick's Kitchen) and the original freight depot. Warm weather dining outside by the tracks. We recommend their subs and soup.

ILLUSIONS - A MAGICAL THEME RESTAURANT
969 Keystone Way (Corner of Keystone and Carmel Dr. -Route 431), **Carmel**

❑ **Area: 4**
❑ Telephone Number: (317) 575-8312
❑ Hours: Monday - Thursday, 5 – 9:00 pm, Friday, 5 - 9:30
   pm, Saturday, 4:30-10:00 pm. Family Summer Magic
   Shows, Saturdays, 6:45 pm. Seating before 5:00 pm.
   Reservations suggested. Average dinner between
   $16 - $25.00.

T he journey begins when you enter and have to remove the sword from the stone...and the giant wall magically opens. One of only 3 magical restaurants where the magic begins as your menu appears out of thin air. Enjoy excellent magic acts at your table after you eat. Be sure to buy a magic menu as your souvenir.

LARRY BIRD'S BOSTON GARDEN RESTAURANT

555 South Third Street, **Terre Haute**

□ **Area: 5**
□ Telephone Number: (800) 255-3399

Walls covered with magazine covers and photos of Larry in action and with other famous folks. Championship banners hang from the ceiling. Glance at his trophies or Olympic gold medal. There's a glass-enclosed area where kids can take a free throw and win a Larry Bird signed certificate. Also a gift shop with Celtic and basketball souvenirs. Try a sandwich called "The Three Pointer" or the "Record Breaker".

MAYBERRY CAFE

78 West Main Street, **Danville**

□ **Area: 6**
□ Telephone Number: (317) 745-4067
□ Hours: Daily, 11:00 am - 10:00 pm

The trip into TV Land starts with Barney's Patrol Car parked out front! As soon as you walk in, you're transformed back to a diner cafe where home-cooked food is served. Many entrees are named after Andy, Opie, Barney, Emmett or maybe Floyd and desserts are Aunt Bea's of course (specialize in cobblers). Aunt Bea says, "If you finish your plate - you get dessert". Each child receives a token redeemable for one toy from Opie's Toy chest or one Opie Sundae. Andy Griffith reruns are played on TV's throughout the diner. Don't miss the autographed photos of the stars on your way back to the Salad Bar.

ACROPOLIS RESTAURANT
1625 East Southport Road, **Indianapolis**

- ❑ **Area: 6**
- ❑ Telephone Number: (317) 787-8883
- ❑ Hours: Monday – Thursday, 11:00 am - 9:30 pm
  Friday - Saturday, 11:00 am – 10:00 pm

F amily-oriented Greek and American menu. Bellydancing on weekend evenings. The whole restaurant gets into it as everyone claps to the beat.

PLANET HOLLYWOOD
130 South Illinois Street, **Indianapolis**

- ❑ **Area: 6**
- ❑ Telephone Number: (317) 822-9222
- ❑ Hours: Lunch / Dinner

W alking up to the restaurant, you'll pass by handprints of famous stars on a concrete wall. Inside you can watch continuous clips while dining to casual fun food like "Home Alone" smoothies or "King Kong" cake for dessert. The best part are the props from famous movies on display. Our kids' favorite: the watch Mr. Slate wore in "The Flintstone's Movie".

NASHVILLE HOUSE
Corner of Main and VanBuren Streets, **Nashville**

- ❑ **Area: 6**
- ❑ Telephone Number: (812) 988-4554
- ❑ Hours: Daily, 11:30 am - 8:00 pm (except Tuesday)
  Friday - Saturday open until 9:00 pm

❑   Miscellaneous: 1859 Historic site with a world-known restaurant famous for fried biscuits and baked apple butter.

THE GASTOF
CR 650 East off US 150, **Montgomery**

❑   **Area: 7**
❑   Telephone Number: (812) 486-3977
❑   Hours: Monday - Saturday. Lunch/Dinner
❑   Tours: By buggy past a harness shop, quilt and craft shop, general store and candy factory.

The restaurant, built of Indiana oak and poplar, was framed by Amish carpenters with simple joints and pegs. Amish cooking.

THE LOG INN
RR 2 I-64 to US 41 East. Turn right on Old State Rd
Warrenton

❑   **Area: 7**
❑   Telephone Number: (812) 867-3216
❑   Hours: Tuesday - Saturday, 4 - 10:00 pm

Built in 1825 as a Noon Day Stage Coach Stop and Trading Post. Dine in the same original Log Room that Abraham Lincoln stopped at in November, 1844 enroute back from visiting his mother's grave. It was part of his campaign speaking tour. Officially recognized as the oldest restaurant in Indiana. Authentic 1-foot thick logs surround you as you eat their wonderful fried chicken meals. Take time to read the articles on the walls while you wait for dinner. Dinners served by a la carte menu or family style.

Chapter 5

ANIMALS & FARMS

FISH HATCHERY - STATE RUN

❑ **Statewide**
❑ Telephone Number: (317) 232-4080. Division of Fish and Wildlife.
❑ Hours: Monday - Friday, 8:00 am - 4:00 pm.
❑ Admission: Free.
❑ Tours: By appointment.
❑ Miscellaneous: Sites are Driftwood (Area 8), Avoca (Area 8), Cikana (Area 6), Fawn River (Area 2), Twin Branch (Area 1), Mix Sawbah (Area 10), and Bass Lake (Area 10).

State run outdoor fish farms produce 200,000 to 1 million fish each year per site. Any of the six farms might raise trout, large mouth bass, blue gill, sunfish, and black crappie for stocking state parks. The caretakers usually start the tour with a slide show; then, it's out to the ponds. You'll be informed about the proper soil and depth of each pond and the vegetation that is most wanted. At the Avoca site, they have more than enough spring water from a cave nearby to supply their thirteen ponds. The best time to visit is harvest time when they drain the pond down to a minimum pool and wade through the water with a sieve to collect fish. In summer and early winter, the rainbow trout are easiest to see as they jump to the surface when you feed them.

BLACK PINE ANIMAL PARK
349 West Albion Road, **Albion**

❑ **Area: 2**
❑ Telephone Number: (219) 636-7383
❑ Hours: Summers only except special events throughout the year. Tuesday - Saturday, 10:00 am - 4:00 pm. Sundays, 1 - 4.00 pm
❑ Admission: Adults $5.00, Children $3.00

❑   Miscellaneous: Feeding tour on Saturday / Sunday at 4:00 pm is $1.00 additional

Animals from around the world which are rescued, rehabilitated or have retired from show business are sent here.

DIEHM MUSEUM OF NATURAL HISTORY
600 Franke Park Drive, **Fort Wayne**

❑   **Area: 2**
❑   Telephone Number: (219) 427-6708
❑   Hours: Wednesday - Sunday, 12 - 5:00 pm.
    (Late April Mid – October)
❑   Admission: Adults $2.00, Children $1.00 (2-12)

North American wildlife mounted in natural settings. There are written and audio descriptions of each exhibit. Also, see displays of minerals and gems.

FORT WAYNE CHILDREN'S ZOO
3411 Sherman Blvd (I-69 to Exit 109A [US 33 South]), **Fort Wayne**

❑   **Area: 2**
❑   Telephone Number: (219) 427-6800
❑   Hours: Daily, 9:00 am - 5:00 pm
    (Late April - Mid October)
❑   Admission: Adults $4.00, Children $3.00
❑   Miscellaneous: Lakeside Gazebo. World's Only Endangered Species Carousel. Tree Tops Cafe.

One of Jack Hanna's "Top 10" favorite zoos in the U.S. is highlighted by:

- ❑ **Indonesian Rain Forest** - Red apes, bats, kimono dragon and giant walking sticks.
- ❑ **African Veldt** - Safari jeep ride on 22 acres of grassland where animals roam free. African village.
- ❑ **Australian Adventure** - Meet a wallaby and her Joey. Great Barrier Reef tropical fish in 20,000 gallon aquarium. Australia After Dark fruit bats. Matilda's Fish and Chips. Herbst River Ride dugout canoe tour. Tasmanian devils. Kangaroos. Parakeets.
- ❑ **Children's Zoo** - petting area. Pony rides. 1860 train ride.
- ❑ **Worms**: Let a centipede crawl up your arm or see worms "worm" through dirt.

WOLF PARK
RR 1 (Head into downtown and follow signs)
Battle Ground

- ❑ **Area: 3**
- ❑ Telephone Number: (765) 567-2265
- ❑ Hours: 1 - 5:00 pm. Best time is weekends. (May – November)
- ❑ Admission: General, $4 - $5.00 (over 13 years)
- ❑ Miscellaneous: Special Wolf-Bison presentations on Sundays at 1:00 pm where they challenge each other's herd. Wolf Howl Nights on Fridays and Saturdays at 7:30 pm - listen to howling, communicating chorus and try to imitate.

You'll see the herd of bison first as you enter (their *faces* are so-o-o large!) and then in another caged area the 3 foxes (the red fox looks just like Todd from "The Fox and The Hound"). A quarter mile walk takes you and your guide to see the packs of gray wolves in actual social structure. See them eat (prepared "recycled" animal road kill), quarrel and rest - at a fairly close distance. Learn why the lower class of wolves always gets picked on. You won't leave without an authentic chorus of howls from the pack. Even in broad daylight, those calls are very eerie! The coyote is always the loudest - showy! Be sure to try to come on weekends when the special programs (see Miscellaneous above) are featured. OW-oool.

GAS CITY MINI ZOO
South Broadway (at Gas City Park off SR 22), Gas City

- **Area: 4**
- Telephone Number: (765) 674-1629
- Hours: Year-round, 7:00 am - 11:00 pm
- Admission: Free
- Miscellaneous: Zoo consists of whitetail deer, sheep, donkeys, mini-horses, llamas, pigmy goats, mute swans, peacocks and poultry. Animal food vending machines available to feed animals.

CANTERBURY ARABIANS
12131 East 196th Street, Noblesville

- **Area: 4**
- Telephone Number: (317) 776-0779
- Hours: Daily 8:00 am - 5:00 pm (call first)
- Admission: Free
- Tours: By appointment

Visit with "Real Mac" – the Indianapolis Colt's Mascot. 50 Arabians at working horse farm. See bathing, eating, or a foal being born. Best visiting time is Spring/Summer when new colts arrive.

ME'S ZOO

CR 500 South, 12441 West Randolph. (Follow sign 4 miles
East on SR 32 to CR 700 East to CR 500), **Parker City**

❑ **Area: 4**
❑ Telephone Number: (765) 468-8559
❑ Hours: Monday – Friday, 10:00 am - 6:00 pm, Saturday,
    10:00 am - 7:00 pm, Sunday, Noon – 7:00 pm
    (May – October)
❑ Admission: Adults $5.50, Children $4.50 (under 12)
❑ Miscellaneous: $0.50 Discount on Wednesday

Privately owned - over 32 acres include a petting area and
picnic/concession area. Small, fenced-in sections give you a
clear view of all the animals. Because it's a "petite zoo", children
(ages 2 - 8 years) enjoy it most (not overwhelming).

JOSEPH MOORE MUSEUM OF
NATURAL HISTORY

Earlham College (US 40 West), **Richmond**

❑ **Area: 4**
❑ Telephone Number: (765) 983-1303
❑ Hours: Monday, Wednesday, Friday, 1 - 4:00 pm
    (September - April), Sunday 1 - 4:00 pm (all year)
❑ Admission: Free
❑ Tours: Staffed by students
❑ Miscellaneous: Ralph Teetor Planetarium - open Sundays

Egyptian mummy and pre-historic animals like a mastodon,
allosaurus skeletons and fossils. Mammals and birds
displayed in natural habitats and typical of Indiana. Hold a LIVE
snake!

INDIANAPOLIS ZOO

1200 West Washington Street (in White River Park), **Indianapolis**

- **Area: 6**
- Telephone Number: (317) 630-2001
- Hours: Daily, 9:00 am - 4:00 pm
  (Seasonal Extended Hours)
- Miscellaneous: Stroller rental. Parking $3.00. Gift shop. FREE from 9:00 am - 12:00 pm - every 1st Tuesday. Reduced prices in winter months.

The 64 acre cageless zoo is home of simulated habitats featuring deserts, plains, forests and the ocean.

- **Neptune Gallery** - well known for the large enclosed whale, sea lion and dolphin pavilions. The only dolphin shows in Indiana are daily at 11:00 am, 1:00 pm and 3:00 pm.
- **Living Deserts of The World** - free roaming desert plants and animals co-exist as they would in nature. Giant Cacti and lizards live under a constant 60-80 degree (F) dome.
- **Encounters Area** - domestic animal shows like Camp Zoorific Magic Show.
- Also, check out the train rides, antique carousel, horse-drawn trolley or pony, camel and elephant rides.

MESKER PARK ZOO

2421 Bement Avenue, off SR 66. (Mesker Park 3 miles North West on St. Joseph Avenue), **Evansville**

- **Area: 7**
- Telephone Number: (812) 428-0715

❑   Hours: Daily, 9:00 am - 4:00 pm (Summer – Weekends
     and Holidays until 7:00 pm).
❑   Admission: Adults $4.75, Children $3.75 (3-12)

Rolling hills area home to approximately 700 animals.
Indiana's largest zoo includes a petting zoo, zoo train, Lake
Victoria paddle boat rides, Discovery Center and Jungle Cafe.
Resident monkeys live in the center of a lake in a concrete replica
of Christopher Columbus' Santa Maria. The zoo is divided into the
African Panorama, Tropical Americas, Asian Valley and North
America.

NEEDMORE BUFFALO FARM AND RESTAURANT

4100 Buffalo Lane (South of SR 62 East - Turn right at sign
and follow signs for 10 miles - between Jefferson and
Corydon), **Elizabeth**

❑   **Area: 8**
❑   Telephone Number: (812) 968-3473
❑   Hours: Daily, 9:00 am – Dark (Except Tuesdays)
❑   Admission: Free
❑   Tours: Adults $4.00, Children $3.00. (12 and under).
     Round-ups by reservation - usually weekends
❑   Miscellaneous: Nanna Jane's Kitchen and Trading Post-
     purchase buffalo meat and crafts.

Large North American bison herd seen during a hayride
through rolling pastures, forests and streams. Learn the role
buffalo played in southern Indiana history. Following Native
American customs, the staff respectfully converts every part of the
buffalo into useful artistic items. Eat in the ranch environment
trying buffalo burgers - very lean... or buffalo jerky. For dessert,

you have to try a buffalo "chip"- pure fudge...no Do Do. The owners are such pleasant folks!

MARY GRAY BIRD SANCTUARY
CR 350 West (3 ½ miles West of SR 121), **Connersville**

- **Area: 9**
- Telephone Number: (765) 825-9788
- Hours: Daily (during daylight hours)
- Admission: Donation
- Miscellaneous: 684 acre nature preserve owned by Indiana Audubon society. Includes foot trails, ponds and a museum.

WASHINGTON PARK ZOO
Lake Shore Drive or Lake Michigan, **Michigan City**

- **Area: 10**
- Telephone Number: (219) 873-1510
- Hours: Vary by season. Daily, 1 - 4:00 pm (except Monday)
- Admission: Adults $2.75, Seniors $2.00 (65+), Children $1.75 (3-11)

A 1928 zoo laid out on the side of a wooded sand dune. One of the oldest and largest zoos with a petting area (near the entrance), children's castle, feline house and monkey island. You also can see the Michigan shoreline and Chicago skyline from the observation tower.

Chapter 6

MUSEUMS

NATIONAL NEW YORK CENTRAL RAILROAD MUSEUM

721 South Main (Right by Amtrak Railroad through town),
Elkhart

❑ **Area: 1**
❑ Telephone Number: (219) 294-3001
❑ Hours: Tuesday - Friday, 10:00 am - 2:00 pm, Saturday, 10:00 am - 4:00 pm, Sunday, Noon - 4:00 pm
❑ Admission: Adults $2.00, Seniors $1.00 (55+), Children $1.00 (6-14)

Trace the railroad heritage of Elkhart through photos, videos of New York trains in action and two model railroad layouts in the 1880's Freight House Museum. Outside is a New York Central "Mohawk" steam locomotive that's very dark black and only slightly restored (it looks like it could tell lots of stories) . There's also an E-8 Diesel and GG-1 Electric locomotive.

HANNAH LINDHAL CHILDREN'S MUSEUM

1402 South Main Street, **Mishawaka**

❑ **Area: 1**
❑ Telephone Number: (219) 254-4540
❑ Tours: Tuesday - Friday, 9:00 am - 4:00 pm, Saturday - Sunday, 10:00 am - 2:00 pm
❑ Admission: General $1.00, Children $0.50 (2-5)

The theme is "Please Do Touch" and kids' eye-level, hands-on exhibits focus on geological history of the area from glaciers to the early 1900's. Touch different surfaces that were affected by the glaciers. View Native American artifacts, tools, clothing, and tee-pees. A Japanese theme room (try on an outfit!) and firefighting equipment and safety.

CIRCUS HALL OF FAME

SR 124 (3 miles East of Peru @ Wallace Circus Winter Quarters), **Peru**

□ **Area: 1**
□ Telephone Number: (765) 472-7553
□ Hours: Monday - Saturday, 10:00 am - 4:00 pm, Sunday, 1 - 4:00 pm (May –October)
□ Admission: Adults $2.50, Children $1.00 (6-12)
□ Miscellaneous: "Summer only" performances (twice daily) are $4 - $6.00 total admission and include calliope concerts, magic circus, animal training and Big Top Circus Shows. Gift Shop.

If you want to see the best of circus life today and days gone-by, you need to go to the source of the most activity in the last 100 years. As you pull up, you'll see the bright Big Top and the sounds of animals and their trainers yelling out commands. In between shows throughout the grounds (see Miscellaneous above), stop over to the Circus Museum. It's located in an old circus barn that served as winter quarters for up to 5 famous traveling shows. Going through the Hall of Fame, you'll recognize greats like Emmett Kelly (classic 1900's clown) and Dan Rice (his act was the character Uncle Sam clown). Our favorites in the museum were the vintage circus wagons, painted colorfully inside and out with closets full of even more brightly colorful costumes.

STUDEBAKER NATIONAL MUSEUM

525 South Main Street (Downtown. Off SR 2 or US 31),
South Bend

❑ **Area: 1**

❑ Telephone Number: (219) 235-9108, (219) 235-9479
(information line)

❑ Hours: Monday - Saturday, 9:00 am - 5:00 pm,
Sunday, Noon - 5:00 pm

❑ Admission: Adults $5.00, Seniors $4.00 Children $2.50
(12 and under)

❑ Miscellaneous: Gift Shop and Science Center Gift Shop.
X90 Hands On Science and Technology Center features
pulleys and fasteners using principles applicable to vehicle
mechanics.

Two Studebaker brothers started supplying wagons to the US
Army for the Civil War and then later W.W.I. Then four
brothers formed a company that grew to be the largest wagon
factory in the world. Their motto was, "Always give more than you
promise". By the 1920's, they were building electric and gasoline-
powered automobiles and continued until closing in 1966. (They
were the only company that built settlers' wagons all the way up to
high performance autos). See the family's Conestoga wagon, a
platinum 1934 Bendix and the last car ever made in South Bend.
There's also an impressive display of carriages belonging to
Presidents Grant, McKinley and Lincoln. The one and only white
Packard Predictor is in the entrance enclosed in a temperature-
controlled case. Can you guess why it has to be in its own case?

BILLY SUNDAY HOME

1111 Sunday Lane and 12th Street (Park Avenue to 12th
Street), **Winona Lake**

- ❑ **Area: 1**
- ❑ Telephone Number: (219) 269-3302
- ❑ Hours: Monday - Saturday, 8:00 am - 5:00 pm
- ❑ Admission: $1.00 (Donation)
- ❑ Tours: By appointment
- ❑ Miscellaneous: Reveals the life of "Ma" and Billy Sunday from the days of his evangelistic crusades to a pro baseball career (uniform and mitt). Listen to a real victrola.

SCIENCE CENTRAL

1950 North Clinton Street, **Fort Wayne**

- ❑ **Area: 2**
- ❑ Telephone Number: (800) 4-HANDS-ON
- ❑ Hours: Tuesday - Saturday, 9:00 am - 5:00 pm, Sunday, Noon - 5:00 pm
- ❑ Admission: Adults $5.00 (13-64 years), Seniors $4.50 (65+), Children $4.00 (3-12)
- ❑ Miscellaneous: Free Parking. Store for Science - affordable science merchandise.

Faces light up from the minute you enter when kids see the middle section of the giant 3 story tube slide! It's the quickest way to go from the 2nd floor to the basement (who needs stairs!). The science/physics playground is housed in the former electric plant. In "Food Foundations", everyone will understand where food comes from and where it goes when you eat it. Kids can also bend rainbows, create tornadoes and earth quakes, become weightless astronauts or ride a bike on a rail 20 feet above ground. There's also a portable planetarium in Starlab and special exhibits like "Bats"- can we be friends?

THE BEN HUR MUSEUM
Crawfordsville

❑ **Area: 3**
❑ Telephone Number: (765) 362-5769. (800) 866-3973
❑ Hours: Wednesday - Saturday, 10:00 am - 4:30 pm,
Sunday, 1:00 - 4:30 pm (Summer)
Tuesday - Sunday, 1 - 5:00 pm (April, May, Sept, October)
❑ Admission: Adults $2.00, Children $0.50 (6-12)
❑ Tours: By appointment year round.

General Lew Wallace built this as his private library and a quiet place where he could write novels such as the famous "Ben Hur." He was also an artist, violinist and inventor. Memorabilia include Wallace's roles as a Civil War general, lawyer, state senator, scholar, and artist.

IMAGINATION STATION
600 North 4th Street & Cincinnati Streets (Downtown),
Lafayette

❑ **Area: 3**
❑ Telephone Number: (765) 420-7780
❑ Hours: Friday - Sunday, 1-5:00 pm
❑ Admission: Adults $3.00, Children $2.00 (3-12)

Hands-on space, science, engineering and technology museum for kids. See and touch a 1920's fire engine, a butterfly house, a 1910 Maxwell auto or a flight simulator.

MUSEUM OF MINIATURE HOUSES

111 East Main Street (I-465 to Keystone, exit North
[US 431] to Main Street), **Carmel**

- ❑ **Area: 4**
- ❑ Telephone Number: (317) 575-9466
- ❑ Hours: Wednesday - Saturday, 11:00 am - 4:00 pm,
  Sunday, 1 - 4:00 pm
- ❑ Admission: Adults $2.00. Children $1.00 (under 10)
- ❑ Miscellaneous: Gift Shop

❝ A world of small things awaits you". Antique and contemporary dollhouses, room boxes, and seasonal displays. Examples: 1861 dollhouse, a large replica of a person's home; a $1/12^{th}$ scale museum within the museum; a house all ready for the daughter's wedding and reception; collections of unique mini accessories.

WILBUR WRIGHT BIRTHPLACE AND MUSEUM

Wilbur Wright Road (just South of US 36 & East of SR 3),
Hagerstown

- ❑ **Area: 4**
- ❑ Telephone Number: (765) 332-2495
- ❑ Hours: Monday - Saturday, 10:00 am - 5:00 pm,
  Sunday, 1 - 5:00 pm (April - October)
- ❑ Admission: Adults $2.00, Children $1.00, Family $5.00
- ❑ Miscellaneous: Gift Shop. Shelter/picnic area. RC air strip

H e and brother, Orville (born later in Dayton) turned the dream of flight into reality. A life-size replica of the Wright Flyer is on display next to the birthplace home of the Wright family filled with memorabilia like shoes and toys.

ELWOOD HAYNES MUSEUM
1915 South Webster Street, **Kokomo**

❑ **Area: 4**
❑ Telephone Number: (765) 456-7500
❑ Hours: Tuesday - Saturday, 1 - 4:00 pm
    Sunday, 1 - 5:00 pm
❑ Admission: Free

Haynes' former residence houses many personal possessions and most interesting, his inventions. He invented "America's First Car" road tested July 4, 1894 on Pumpkinville Pike. See the first stellite cobalt-based alloy discovered in 1906 while searching for metal to make new tableware and in the same process, he invented stainless steel. The tarnish-free dinnerware was developed to satisfy Mrs. Haynes' request.

CHILDREN'S MUSEUM
515 South High Street (off I-69 to CR 67, Downtown),
Muncie

❑ **Area: 4**
❑ Telephone Number: (765) 286-1660
❑ Hours: Tuesday - Saturday, 10:00 am - 5:00 pm
    Sunday, 1 - 5:00 pm
❑ Admission: General $4.00 (ages 1-100 years)
❑ Miscellaneous: Gift Shop. Annual membership available

This hands-on museum is designed to stimulate curiosity and imagination. Older kids may want to head straight upstairs where they can hold small animals and snakes or to the Outdoor Learning Center. Experience Indiana from several points of view - a forest treehouse, a farm and pond or a limestone quarry that produces materials that build giant columns. Younger ones will gravitate to the dress-up clothes (ants, ladybugs) and take the challenge of climbing through a giant ant hill. Next, they might build a sand castle, play with waterways or pretend to be a storekeeper in a simulated town with play props. After you take a picture or two on the full-size tractor or in the cab of a semi-truck, leave enough time for the best display - Garfield. This is the only permanent Garfield display in the world (could be here because creator Jim Davis lives in Muncie). School-aged kids will want to try to make their own Garfield cartoon strip with help (video interactive) from Jim Davis. The highlight of our trip had to be co-starring in a short Garfield cartoon. For a small fee, you can record this family treasure (all of our relatives have seen this at least once) of members of your family zapped into a Garfield skit and actually interacting with him. As you watch in a monitor, Garfield casually instructs you to jump, dance, stop or run with him. It's a blast!

ERNIE PYLE STATE HISTORIC SITE
SR 71 Downtown (1 mile North of US 36), **Dana**

- ❑ **Area: 5**
- ❑ Telephone Number: (317) 665-3633
- ❑ Hours: Tuesday - Saturday, 9:00 am - 5:00 pm
  Sunday, 1 - 5 pm. (Mid-March – December)
- ❑ Admission: Free

Summed up by a plaque saying, "At this spot, the 77th Infantry Division lost a Buddy, Ernie Pyle, 18 April, 1945". An endearing man who wrote an aviation column for the Washington Daily News and then became a roving reporter traveling the country. He wrote of ordinary people who had a simple story to tell. In 1940, Pyle went to report on the war in Europe and America's involvement. During that assignment, he was shot by a Japanese soldier.

CHILDREN'S SCIENCE AND TECHNOLOGY MUSEUM
523 Wabash Avenue, Terre Haute

- ❏ **Area: 5**
- ❏ Telephone Number: (812) 235-5548
- ❏ Hours: Tuesday - Saturday, 9:00 am - 4:00 pm
- ❏ Admission: Adults $2.50, Seniors $2.00, Children $2.00 (3-12)

Small museum has hands-on science like: a shadow wall, lasers, a stoplight, model trains, holograms, fossils, a TV studio, marble races and a dinosaur nest (by the front window - play pretend).

FIRE AND POLICE MUSEUM
Eighth and Idaho Streets, Terre Haute

- ❏ **Area: 5**
- ❏ Telephone Number: (812) 235-9865
- ❏ Hours: Daily, 1 - 4:00 pm (May - Mid-September)
- ❏ Admission: Free

1840's equipment like the 1st motorized fire truck used in Indiana and uniforms, badges, first-aid equipment and guns. Upstairs is a sample dorm with boots and pants laid out in case the alarm sounds and a fireman has to dress quickly to slide down the fire pole (also on display) in a flash!

MATHERS' MUSEUM
416 North Indiana Avenue (Northwest side of Indiana University Campus), Bloomington

- ❏ **Area: 6**
- ❏ Telephone Number: (812) 855-MUSE

- ❏ Hours: Tuesday - Friday, 9:00 am - 4:30 pm, Saturday - Sunday, 1 - 4:30 pm. Closed during semester breaks.
- ❏ Admission: Free
- ❏ Tours: Recommended. Guides bring the interactive displays to life.
- ❏ Miscellaneous: Gift shop with items as low as $0.50. We'd recommend that each child purchase a different, unusual musical instrument to form a cultural band when they get home.

2 0,000 artifacts from across the world reveal traditions, values and beliefs in objects people create and use every day. Kids hands-on area has a pretend house in a Greek Village where you can dress up Grecian and play house. After learning about and sampling their huge ethnic instrument collection (our favorite part), ask the guide for assistance in making one of your own using recycled everyday materials.

JAMES WHITCOMB RILEY OLD HOME AND MUSEUM 250
West Main Street (I-70 to SR 9 to US 40), **Greenfield**

- ❏ **Area: 6**
- ❏ Telephone Number: (765) 462-8539
- ❏ Hours: Tuesday – Saturday, 10:00 am - 4:00 pm
  Sunday 1 - 4:00 pm (May – October)
- ❏ Tours: Every half hour

M r. Riley was born in Greenfield in 1849 and his 1044 poems brought him the name, Hoosier Poet. (They are mostly about Indiana and kids). Famous characters he developed were the Raggedy Man, Little Orphan Annie and Old Aunt Mary from people he talked with and observed and events like the circus in town or a harvest festival. Best part of the tour is the winding, creaky staircase, rafter room, cubby-hole and chimney flue. All part of ghost stories. Little Orphan Annie "used to tell stories that always ended "Er the Gobble-uns'll get you-ef you don't watch out!" (Our guide recited several of these adapted-story poems with us throughout the tour - it was a delightful way to add mystique to a very simple home).

THE CHILDREN'S MUSEUM

3000 North Meridian Street (30th Street between Meridian and Illinois Streets - SR 37 North), **Indianapolis**

❑ **Area: 6**
❑ Telephone Number: (317) 924-KIDS
❑ Hours: Monday - Saturday, 10:00 am - 5:00 pm
    Sunday, Noon - 5:00 pm, (Memorial Day - Labor Day)
    (Closed Mondays rest of year)
❑ Admission: Adults $8.00, Seniors $7.00 (60+)
    Children $3.50 (2-17)
❑ Miscellaneous: Free admission 1st Thursday, 5 - 8:00 pm.
    Annual passes available. IWERKS Cinedome - 3 story
    theatre makes you feel you're part of action - like being in
    a parade or hot air balloon. Separate admission

B e sure that your kids have a good nap or plan multiple visits cause this place is full of 5 floors of fun! This place is as good as they say it is – a must visit! The largest and most popular children's museum in the world includes these favorite areas:

❑ **The Largest Water Clock in the World** - Located at
    entrance and a marvel to watch-looks like a giant science
    fair project.
❑ **Passport to the World** - Cultures and people. Look
    through cutouts facing a mirror to see yourself dressed
    as a kid from another country or try your hand at playing
    foreign instruments or watching a performance.

- **Trains:** Locomotives sight and sound train depot shows really sound and feel like the trains is leaving the station.
- **Playscape** - Baby area with super soft play/crawl area and water, sand, garden, dress up, play house, areas for pre-schoolers.
- **Space Quest Planetarium** - 3 D flight and simulated star. Projection laser light shows to modern "hip" music and characters ("Garfield")
- **Egyptian Tomb** - A 2700 year old real mummy with walk-along displays that teach you materials and scents used to prepare the body.
- **Science Works** - Send the pre-schoolers over to Playscape. School-aged children are hands-on with the Dock Shop multi-station water learning and construction site with stations where kids (using safe, scaled down material) pretend and play in all phases of constructing a new building.
- **Miscellaneous** - Dinosaurs, Indiana Jones archeology dig, antique carousel.

HOOK'S HISTORICAL DRUG STORE

1202 East 38th Street (on the Indiana State Fairgrounds off SR 37 North), **Indianapolis**

- **Area: 6**
- Telephone Number: (317) 924-1503
- Hours: Daily, 11:00 am - 5:00 pm, (July – August) Tuesday – Sunday, 11:00 am - 5:00 pm (rest of year)
- Admission: Free

Museum displays antique dental, medical, and pharmaceutical equipment. Original furnished operating soda fountain. Sit at the counter of a turn-of-the century drug store. To feel the nostalgia, try a cherry phosphate in a souvenir glass (bubbly but not sugary sweet). Cash registers are still the antique crank-operated kind. Museum also has collections of antique bubble gum machines and baby bottles. Founded in 1900, Hook's Drug Stores were one of the oldest chains until it was bought by Revco in 1994. It's the only Hook's left in the nation. Learn how to make homemade cough syrup with ingredients available at Hook's.

DR. TED'S MUSICAL MARVELS
I-64 (Exit 57 to US 231 North), Dale

❑   **Area: 7**
❑   Telephone Number: (812) 937-4250
❑   Hours: Daily, (Memorial Day - Labor Day). Weekends in May & September.
❑   Admission: Adults $4.50, Children $2.00 (6-12)
❑   Tours: Guided tour of wonderful collection of restored mechanical musical instruments including music boxes, street organs, nickelodeons. Takes you back in time to the hey day of amusement parks and carousels. Actually, hear them played. Gift shop.

EVANSVILLE MUSEUM
411 SE Riverside Drive (Downtown in Sunset Park), Evansville

❑   **Area: 7**
❑   Telephone Number: (812) 425-2406
❑   Hours: Tuesday - Saturday, 10:00 am - 5:00 pm
    Sunday, Noon - 5:00 pm
❑   Admission: Free. (Donations)
❑   Miscellaneous: Museum Shop. Collection of artwork from the 16th century to the present and an Anthropology gallery

on the two upper levels. Koch Planetarium - weekends for small fee.

❑ **"Rivertown USA"** - Main street in the late 1800's. Included are Doctors' and dentists' offices (after looking at those old-style tools they used, it's a wonder that anyone ever went for medical help). The doctor's diploma was received after only 4 months of instruction! Also in the town, was a cute Tim Horn Toy Store with play furniture, blocks, spinning tops and soldiers.

❑ **The Transportation Center** – "EMTRAC" focuses on modes of early transport - dugout canals, steam boats, autos, and steam locomotives.

❑ **"Family Place"** and **"Science Discovery Forest"** - are science centers for school-aged and pre-school kids. Family Place has hands-on exhibits dealing with lasers, optical illusions, gravity and spatial relationships - all very applicable to everyday situations. The Forest is a hands-on forest of speaking tubes, create your-own rolling ball game or rubber band art, water play, a GIANT stuffed bear and a treehouse with manual toy games like LEGOS.

ALYCE BARTHOLOMEW CHILDREN'S MUSEUM
2921 Franklin Street, **Michigan City**

❑ **Area: 10**
❑ Telephone Number: (219) 874-8222
❑ Hours: Saturday, 10:00 am - 4:00 pm
❑ Admission: Adults $3.50, Students $2.50
❑ Tours: By appointment (weekdays)

❑   Miscellaneous: This tudor home has 12 exhibit areas.
    Hands-on, interactive exhibits explore science principles,
    nature, sounds, music, color, light and culture.

OLD LIGHTHOUSE MUSEUM
Heisman Harbor Road, **Michigan City**

❑   **Area: 10**
❑   Telephone Number: (219) 872-6133
❑   Hours: Daily, 1 - 4:00 pm (except Monday)
❑   Admission: General $2.00, Children $1.50
    (12 and younger)

An original 1858 lighthouse filled with displays of recreated keeper's house, lake lore, ship wrecks, and maritime history. Take the cat walk out to the only operational lighthouse in Indiana. Learn how the lighthouse keeper and his/her family (the most famous keeper was a woman) lived and worked.

PORTER COUNTY OLD JAIL MUSEUM
152 South Franklin Street, **Valparaiso**

❑   **Area: 10**
❑   Telephone Number: (219) 465-3595
❑   Hours: Saturday/Sunday/Wednesday, 1 - 4:00 pm
❑   Admission: Free.
❑   Miscellaneous: Old jail. World War II pectoral marquetry
    artwork. Wild West Bronco John (Buffalo Bill's partner).
    Dresses from Inaugural Ball of Abe Lincoln.

Chapter 7

OUTDOOR EXPLORING

GENERAL INFORMATION

BICYCLING

❏   Indiana Bicycle Coalition. (800) BIKE-110
❏   Hoosier Bikeway System. Department of Natural Resources. (317) 232-9200.

CAMPING

❏   Hoosier Camper Guide. (800) 837-7842.

CANOEING

❏   Get Out & Go Guide. Tourism Division. (317) 232-8860.

FALL COLOR

❏   Peak Fall Color Leaf Line. Department of Natural Resources. (317) 232-4002.

FARM MARKETS

❏   Indiana Farm Markets. Get Out & Go Guides. Office of Commissioner of Agriculture. (317) 232-8770.

HIKING

❏   Get Out & Go Guide. Tourism Division. (317) 232-8860.

HORSEBACK RIDING

❏   Get Out & Go Guide. Tourism Division. (317) 232-8860.

HUNTING & FISHING

❏   Division of Fish and Wildlife. (317) 232-4080.

RECREATION

❏   Indiana Recreation Guide. Department of Natural Resources. (800) 622-4931.

SKIING

❏   Ski Paoli Peaks. Paoli. (812) 723-4696.
❏   Perfect North Slopes. Lawrenceburg. (812) 537-3754.

COUNTY PARKS & RECREATION DEPARTMENTS

- ❑ Adams County Parks. (219) 724-2520
- ❑ Carmel – Clay County Parks & Recreation (317) 848-7275.
- ❑ Cass County Parks & Recreation (219) 753-2928.
- ❑ Cicero Department of Parks & Recreation (317) 984-3475.
- ❑ Fishers Department of Parks & Recreation (317) 595-3155.
- ❑ Fort Wayne Parks Department (219) 427-6000.
- ❑ Hamilton County Department Of Parks & Recreation (317) 896-3811.
- ❑ Indianapolis Parks & Recreation (317) 327-0000.
- ❑ Kokomo Parks & Recreation (317) 452-0063.
- ❑ LaPorte County Parks. (219) 326-6808.
- ❑ Luhr County Parks. (219) 324-5855.
- ❑ Monroe County Parks & Recreation (812) 349-2800.
- ❑ Muncie/Delaware County Parks. (765) 747-4858.
- ❑ Noblesville Parks & Recreation (317) 776-6350.
- ❑ Richmond Parks & Recreation (765) 983-7275.
- ❑ Tippecanoe County Parks. (765) 463-2306.

DEPARTMENT OF NATURAL RESOURCES

STATE PARKS/RESERVOIRS

- • (317) 232-4124 OR (800) 622-4931

ENTRANCES

DNR properties that charge admission have the following fees:

- • $2.00 Vehicle Gate Fee (in state plates)

- $5.00 Vehicle Gate Fee (out of state plates)
- $18.00 Annual Entrance Permit (in state)
- $25.00 Annual Entrance Permit (out of state)
- $9.00 Golden Hoosier Passport

RENT-A-TENT

At Tippecanoe State Park, the Class "B" campsite is $7.00 per night (a $25 deposit required). Campsite includes a canvas tent mounted on a wood platform, a camp stove, lantern, cooler, cots (foam pads available) and a picnic table with a fire ring.

STATE PARKS

Most State Parks offer the following facilities: Bicycle Trail, Boating, Camping, Cross-Country Skiing, Cultural Arts Programs, Fishing, Hiking, Nature Center, Picnicking and Equipment Rentals. Other additional facilities specific to each park are listed.

POTATO CREEK

1 – North Liberty. 25601 St. Rd. 4. (219) 656-8186. Bridle Trails, Cabins, Swimming/Beach.

CHAIN O'LAKES

1 - 2355 East 75 South, off SR 9. (219) 636-2654. Eight connecting lakes, Swimming/Beach.

POKAGON

2 - **Angola**. 450 Lane 100 Lake James. (219) 833-2012. Potawatomi Inn. (219) 833-1077. Accommodations and Restaurant, Swimming/Beach, Indoor Pool/Whirlpool, Tennis, Toboggan Run operating Thanksgiving Day through February with track speeds of 35-40 mph.

OUBACHE

2 – Bluffton. 4930 East St. Rd. 201. (219) 824-0926. On the Wabash River. Swimming Pool with Waterslide, Tennis and Basketball Courts.

SHADES

3 – Waveland. SR 1, Off SR 47. (765) 435-2810. Sandstone cliffs, Adjacent Pine Hills Nature Preserve.

MOUNDS

4 - Just east of **Anderson.** 4306 Mounds Road, I-69 to CR 320 to CR 232. (765) 642-6627. The park features 10 distinct "earthworks" built by a group of prehistoric Indians known as the Adena-Hopewell people. The largest earthwork, the "Great Mound", is believed to have been constructed around 160 BC. It's a circular enclosure almost ¼ mile in circumference. Stand in the middle and catch the feeling of Ancient tribal ceremonies that might have been held. The nature center is located in the Bronnenberg House, which is one of the oldest buildings in the County and was built from materials in the surrounding woods. Bridle Trails, Swimming/Pool.

SUMMIT LAKE

4 - New Castle. 5993 North Messick Road, Off US 36. (765) 766-5873. Class A camp lots, Swimming/Beach bathhouse.

SHAKAMAK

5 – Jasonville. 6265 W. SR 48. (812) 665-2158. 400 acres of water, Swimming/Pool with waterslide, Tennis.

TURKEY RUN

5 – Marshall. US 41 to SR 47. (765) 597-2635. Turkey Run Inn (765) 597-2211. Accommodations with indoor pool. Rock-walled canyons and gorges along Sugar Creek, Colonel Richard Lieber Cabin, Planetarium, Tennis & other Games.

MCCORMICK'S CREEK

5 – Spencer. CR 46 near CR 43. (812) 829-2235. Canyon Inn (812) 829-4881 Accommodations. Unique limestone formations and scenic waterfalls along the White River, Swimming/Pool.

FORT HARRISON

6 – Indianapolis. 5753 Glenn Road, Off I-465 & 56th Street. (317) 591-0904. The Fort - (317) 543-9597. Golf Resort and Harrison House Suites & 3 Officer's Home plus dining. Large hardwood forest.

WHITE RIVER STATE PARK

6 – Indianapolis (Downtown). (800) 665-9056. A half mile Riverwalk Promenade made of Indiana limestone offers beautiful waterways, lots of grassy areas and tree-lined boulevards. Pumphouse Visitors Center, IMAX 3D Theater, Eiteljorg Museum of American Indians and Western Art, The Indianapolis Zoo, Victory Field and The National Institute for Fitness and Sport.

BROWN COUNTY

6 – Nashville. CR 46. (812) 988-6406. Cabins & Abe Martin Lodge. (812) 988-4418. Accommodations and Restaurant. Bridle Trails, Swimming Pool, Tennis & Other Games, Yellowwood State Forest (rare trees). T.C. Steele State Memorial (812) 988-2785. The large studio with paintings of Hoosier scenes and the House of Singing Woods.

LINCOLN

7 – Lincoln City. I – 64 to US 231 to CR 162. (812) 937-4710. See listing for Lincoln Boyhood National Memorial in the History Chapter.

HARMONIE

7 - New Harmony. Off CR 69, on the banks of the Wabash.. (812) 682-4821. Known for their trails, Swimming/Pool with Waterslide.

CHARLESTOWN

8 - Charlestown. Off SR 62. (812) 256-5600. Rugged terrain hiking, Devonian fossils, Bird Watchers.

FALLS OF THE OHIO

8 – Clarksville. I – 65 Exit 0, follow signs. (812) 280-9970. The "Age of Fish" coral reef fossil beds are among the largest exposed Devonian fossil beds in the world. The park features a spectacular visitor center overlooking the fossil beds containing an exhibit and video presentation. While fossil collecting is prohibited, visitors are free to explore – we could identify corals, sponges, sea shells and snails. The months of August through October are the most accessible as the river is at its lowest level. Tip: It was suggested to splash water on a colony area and they will "jump out" showing exquisite detail.

SPRING MILL

8 – Mitchell. SR 37 to SR 60East. (812) 849-4129. Spring Mill Inn (812) 849-4081 - Accommodations and Restaurant. Restored Pioneer Village includes a gristmill, lime kiln, sawmill, hat shop, post office, apothecary and boot shop. Twin Cave or Donaldson Cave. Grissom Memorial honors Hoosier astronaut "Gus" Grissom, one of seven Mercury astronauts and America's second man in space. A space capsule and video of space exploration. Swimming/Pool, Tennis & other games.

WHITEWATER MEMORIAL

9 – Liberty. 1418 S SR 101. (765) 458-5565. Bridle Trails, Swimming/Beach.

CLIFTY FALLS

9 - Madison. Off SR 62 or 56. (812) 265-1331. Clifty Inn (812) 265-4135 Accommodations and Restaurant. Swimming/Pool with waterslide, Tennis & other games.

VERSAILLES

9 – Versailles. US 50. (812) 689-6424. Bridle Trails, Swimming/Pool and waterslide.

INDIANA DUNES

10 – Chesterton. Kemil Road at US 12, 3 miles East of SR 49. (219) 926-1952. Buell Memorial Nature Center offers a 12 minute video about dunes and surrounding plant life that is helpful to watch before exploring. The largest "live" dune, Mt. Baldy ("live" means it still moves as wind lifts grains of sand & drops them) is guaranteed to make your mouth drop and your eyes open wide. It's a thrill to climb quickly to the top (123 ft.) and let the dune slide you down to the water's edge. (Note to Parents: be ready for an aerobic workout!). On a windy day, place a beach toy on the sand and watch a mini-dune form behind it! On a windy day you can also hear the sand "sing" under your feet – it's true! Swimming/Beach.

BASS LAKE STATE BEACH

10 – Knox. 5838 SR 10. (219) 772-3382. Summer and (219) 946-3213 Winter. Partially shaded beach and bathhouse, Water-skiing.

TIPPECANOE RIVER

10 – Winamac. 4200 North US 35. (219) 946-3213. Bridle trails, Canoeing, Rent-A-Tent.

STATE RESERVOIRS

Most facilities offer the following services: Boating, Camping, Cultural Arts Programs, Fishing, Hiking, Hunting, Interpretive & Recreational Programs, Picnicking, Playgrounds, Rentals – fishing boats, pontoons, Swimming/Beach, Water-skiing.

SALAMONIE LAKE

1 – Andrews. 9214 West Lost Bridge West. (219) 468-2124. Bridle Trails, Basketball and Volleyball on beach, Cross-country skiing, Nature Center, Snowmobile Trails.

MISSISSINEWA LAKE

1 – Peru. RR 1 (765) 473-6528. Basketball Court, Horseshoes, Volleyball, Frisbee Golf Course, Radio Control Flying Field.

HUNTINGTON LAKE

2 – Huntington. J. Edward Roush Lake. 517 North Warren Road off Rt. 5. (219) 468-2165. Archery Range, Basketball Courts, Mountain Bike Trail, Horseshoes & Croquet, Model Airport, Volleyball Courts on beach.

CAGLES MILL LAKE

5 – Cloverdale. 1317 West Lieber Road, Lieber State Recreation Area. (765) 795-4576. Activity Center, Water Safari Boat Tours.

CECIL M. HARDEN LAKE

5 – Rockville. 160 South Raccoon State Recreation Area. (765) 344-1412. Archery, Basketball Courts, Horseshoe Pits, Volleyball Courts.

MONROE LAKE

6 – Bloomington. 4850 South SR 446. (812) 837-9546. Nature Center, Volleyball Courts.

PATOKA LAKE

8 – Birdseye. RR 1. (812) 685-2464. Archery range, Frisbee Golf Course, Solar Heated Visitors Center.

HARDY LAKE

8 – Scottsburg. 4171 East Harrod Road. (812) 794-3800. Archery Range, Various Sport Courts.

BROOKVILLE LAKE

9 – Brookville. US 27 to SR 101 South. (765) 647-2658. Archery, Horseshoe Pits, Shooting Range, Volleyball.

STATE FORESTS

All forests offer the following: Boating, Camping, Cultural Arts Programs, Fishing, Hiking, Picnicking, Boat rentals and Swimming.

OWEN-PUTNAM

5 – Spencer. RR 4. (812) 829-2462. Bridle Trails.

MORGAN-MONROE

6 - Martinsville. 6220 Forest Road. (765) 342-4026.

YELLOWWOOD

6 – Nashville. 772 South Yellowwood Road. (812) 988-7945. Bridle Trails, Visitors Center.

DEAM LAKE

7 - Borden. 1217 Deam Lake Road, SR 60. (812) 246-5421.

FERDINAND

7 – Ferdinand. 6583 East SR 264. (812) 367-1524.

MARTIN

7 – Shoals. (812) 247-3491.

JACKSON-WASHINGTON

8 – Brownstown. 1278 East SR 250. (812) 358-2160. Skyline View, Archery Range, Basketball and Volleyball Courts, Bridle Trails.

HARRISON CRAWFORD / WYANDOTTE COMPLEX

8 – Corydon. 7240 Old Forest Road SW bordering the Ohio River. (812) 738-8232. Bridle Trails.

CLARK

8 - Henryville. (812) 294-4306. Seven Fishing Lakes, Bridle Trails.

STARVE HOLLOW

8 - Vallonia. 4345 South CR 275 West. (812) 358-3464. Volleyball, Softball & Basketball.

SELMIER

9 – North Vernon. 905 East CR 350 North. (812) 346-2286. Limited facilities.

PIKE

9 - Winslow. 2310 East SR 364. (812) 789-2724. Bridle Trails.

GARDENS AND ARBORETUMS

SHIOJIRI NIWA GARDENS

1 – Mishawaka. Large plants and boulders.

WARSAW BIBLICAL GARDENS

1 – Warsaw. 313 South Buffalo (SR 15). (219) 267-6419. ¾ acre contains trees, flowers, herbs and plants mentioned in the Bible. Dawn to dusk. (Mid-April to Mid-October)

FOELLINGER-FREIMANN BOTANICAL CONSERVATORY

2 – Fort Wayne. 1100 South Calhoun Street (near Jefferson Street, downtown). (219) 427-6440. Even the lobby invites you to a tropical paradise as you browse over your map. Stop in the Tulip Tree Gift Shop that entices you to escape the stone and brick of the city for "gardens under glass". Their showcase display has changing seasons (mums in the Fall, Poinsettias at the Holidays, daffodils in the Spring) along with the permanent Desert House and Tropical House. Did you know a banana tree bears fruit once and then dies? Monday – Saturday, 10:00 am – 5:00 pm, Sunday Noon – 4:00 pm. $1.25 - $2.50.

CLEGG BOTANICAL GARDENS

3 – Lafayette. 1782 North 400 East. (765) 423-1325. One mile walk includes wildflowers, 250 plants and a view from Lookout Point. Daily, 10:00 am – Sunset. Free.

MORRIS-ELLIS CONSERVATORY

4 – Anderson. 35,000 annuals grown here for area parks.

CHRISTY WOODS

4 – Muncie. Ball State University. Between Riverside and University Avenues. (765) 285-8820. 17 acres with nature center: Wheeler Orchid Collection has the most variety in the world. No Admission. (April – October)

OAKHURST GARDENS

4 – Muncie. Minnetrista Culture Center. (800) 4 – CULTURE. Home and garden of elegant Victorian heiress to Ball Corporation canning jars. Discovery Cabin for the kids to explore nature hands-on. Tuesday – Saturday, 10:00 am – 5:00 pm. Sunday, 1 – 5:00 pm.

HAYES REGIONAL ARBORETUM

4 – Richmond. 801 Elks Country Club Road. (765) 962-3745. 355 acre nature preserve with 179 woody plants native to the region. 1st solar greenhouse. Old 1833 Dairy Barn Nature Center with exhibits, gift shop and bird sanctuary. Tuesday – Saturday, 9:00 am – 5:00 pm. Sunday, 1 – 5:00 pm. No Admission.

GARFIELD PARK CONSERVATORY

6 – Indianapolis. 2450 South Shelby Street. (317) 784-3044. Paved paths travel past a 15 foot waterfall and 500 tropical plants like orchids, palms and cactuses. Tuesday – Saturday, 10:00 am – 5:00 pm. Sunday, Noon – 5:00 pm. No Admission.

HOLLIDAY PARK

6 – Indianapolis. 6349 Spring Mill Road. 50 acre arboretum with more than 800 varieties of trees and plants.

WESSELMAN WOODS NATURE PRESERVE

7 – Evansville. 551 North Boeke Road. (I-164 to SR 66). (812) 479-0771. 200 acres of bottomland hardwood forest, fields and ponds. Nature Center has trail maps, lists of wildflowers, birds and trees to look for and brochures covering maple sugaring, pioneer skills and forestry.

CAVERNS AND CAVES

BLUESPRING CAVERNS PARK

Bluespring Caverns Road. (US 50 and SR 37 on CR 450 South) **Bedford**

- ❑ **Area: 8**
- ❑ Telephone Number: (812) 279-9471

❑ Hours: Daily, 9:00 am – 5:00 pm. (Memorial Day – Labor
    Day, Weekends only, (April, May, September & October)
    EST.

❑ Admission: Adults $9.00, Children $5.00 (3-15)

❑ Miscellaneous: Always a 52 degree constant temperature –
    a light jacket recommended. Myst'ry River Gemstone
    Mine – prospect for your own gemstones. "Overnight
    Adventures" for organized youth groups.

Y ears ago the White River cut into small cracks in limestone
    rock and dissolved it forming cave passages. As glaciers
moved into the area they brought debris of soil and rock that were
deposited. In the 1940's, a large pond on a farm disappeared
overnight to reveal the entrance to the cave. The Myst'ry River
tour boat glides along the quiet waters. The guide will point out
unusual formations and the interesting albino blind fish and
crawfish that live in darkness.

SQUIRE BOONE CAVERNS AND VILLAGE

SR 135 South. I – 64 exit 105. Watch for signs (some pretty
funny). **Corydon**

❑ **Area: 8**

❑ Telephone Number: (502) 425-CAVE or (812) 732-4381

❑ Hours: 10:00 am – 5:00 pm. (Memorial Day – Labor Day)
    Pre-scheduled the rest of the year between 10:00 am – 4:00
    pm every two hours.

❑ Admission: Adults $9.50, Children $4.50 (ages 5 +)

❑ Tours: Last one hour every 30 minutes. Group packages
    include hayrides and bonfires.

❑ Miscellaneous: Boones 1804 Mill – bakery, Gem mining
    (fossils and gems), soap and candlemaking, petting zoo
    and playground (Summer only). Caverns are a constant 54
    degrees year round. A light jacket is suggested.

Explore the same caverns that Squire and Daniel Boone discovered in 1790 as Squire was out searching for his older brother, Daniel who had been captured by hostile Indians. Walk past stalactites, stalagmites, blind and albino crayfish, underground streams and waterfalls, dams and the foundation stone carved by Squire himself. It's all very quiet. Squire's life was spared when he hid in the caverns from a band of pursuing Indians – he is even buried in his beloved cave. Buy a spelunking explorer hat with light for the kids to use while they tour. Then they have a great souvenir that was actually used at the site.

WYANDOTTE CAVES

I – 64 to SR 66 South to SR 62 East, **Leavenworth**

- ❑ **Area: 8**
- ❑ Telephone Number: (812) 738-2782
- ❑ Hours: Daily, 9:00 am – 5:00 pm. EDST. Closed Mondays in winter (mid-September to mid-May).
- ❑ Admission: Adults $ 4 – $5.00, Children $2 –$2.50
- ❑ Tours: 30 minute to 2 hour trips
- ❑ Miscellaneous: Children 12 and under must be with an adult. Caves are a constant 52 degrees.
  - Little Wyandotte Tour – short and easy with flowstone and dripstone formations. Indirect electrical lighting.
  - Big Wyandotte Historical Tours – Rugged Mountain, geologic historical formations. Summer only. Prehistoric Indian "rooms" and "hallways".
  - Monument Mountain Tour – deep cave with formations like helictites, gypsum/flint quarries. 1 1/2 miles of steep terrain and stairs.

MARENGO CAVE

I – 64 to SR 66 and SR 64, **Marengo**

- ❑ **Area: 8**
- ❑ Telephone Number: (812) 365-2705
- ❑ Hours: Daily, 9:00 am – 5:00 pm. (Summer)
  9:30 am – 5:30pm EST. (Spring and Fall)
  9:00 am – 5:00 pm (Winter)
- ❑ Admission: Adults $9.50+, Children $4.75+ (4–12)
- ❑ Tours: Leave every 30 minutes
- ❑ Miscellaneous: Hungry Grotto Snack Shop. Cave Springs
  Mining Company – gemstone mining – Daily, (April –
  October). Climbing Tower. Canoe trips, trail rides.

- Crystal Palace Tour – 40 minutes, world famous
  "Crystal Palace" cave room with dramatic lighting
  presentation. Mountain rooms and massive deposits.
- Dripstone Trail Tour – One hour and 10 minutes.
  Known for sodastraw formations, slender and
  intricate " dripping" deposits. Includes "Pulpit
  Rock", "Music Hall" and "Penny Ceiling".
- The Crawl – challenging, simulated cave maze
  crawl. Do you have what it takes to be a cave
  explorer? Physically fit ages 8 – 30 only.
  Claustrophobia City! Best to try before the Cave
  Exploring trip is purchased.
- Cave Exploring Trips – age 10 and up. Don a
  lighted helmet and old clothes and crawl through
  undeveloped new cave passages. Be sure to get a
  picture of yourself on this excursion. Friends won't
  believe it!

WHITEWATER GORGE PARK
64 Waterfall Road at Brookville Lake.
(2200 US 40 East), **Liberty**

- **Area: 9**
- Telephone Number: (765) 983-7275
- Hours: Daily Dawn to Dusk
- Admission: Free

Fossil collecting with geologic information available to play pretend archeologists. The Gorge formed during the Ice Age and has many vertical cliffs surrounding Thistlewaite Falls.

GUSE CHRISTMAS TREE FARM
6177 West 1450 South, **Wanatah**

- **Area: 10**
- Telephone Number: (219) 733-2213
- Hours: Monday – Saturday (call ahead, please)
- Admission: Free
- Tours: By appointment. 45 minutes long. (Mid-November to Mid-December).

3rd and 4th generation year round business raising Christmas trees. 125 acres of trees show how different trees grow, how Christmas wreaths are made, and the operations it takes to make the finest trees.

Chapter 8

ARTS & ENTERTAINMENT

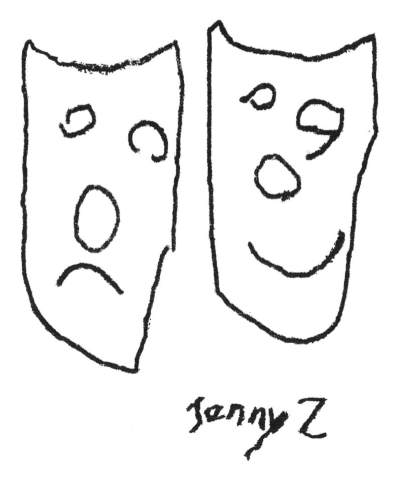

Janny Z

- INDIANA ARTS COMMISSION. (317) 232-1268
- INDIANA ARTS COUNCIL. (800) 965-ARTS
- ARTS INDIANA INC. (317) 686-2250

SOUTH BEND REGIONAL MUSEUM OF ART

1 – South Bend. Century Center, 120 South St. Joseph Street. (219) 235-9102. Arts Education Center with classes and galleries.

WAGON WHEEL THEATRE

1 - Warsaw. (219) 267-8041. In-The-Round stage performances of children's productions.

BEARCREEK FARMS

2 – Bryant. 8339 North 400 East. Off US 27. (800) 288-7630. Children's Theatre, Saturdays at 10:00 am. Country Fair - carousel, kiddie rides, train rides, mini-golf. Small admission. Red Barn Restaurant converted from a real barn. (Mid-May to Mid-September)

FORT WAYNE MUSEUM OF ART

2 - Fort Wayne. 311 East Main Street. (219) 422-6467. Contemporary art. Tuesday - Saturday, 10:00 am - 5:00 pm, Sunday, Noon - 5:00 pm. Hands-on for Kids' Education at Eckrich Gallery.

ANDERSON CHILDREN'S CHOIR

4 - Anderson.

ANDERSON YOUNG BALLET THEATRE AND ACADEMY

4 - Anderson. Sample plays include "Cinderella" and "The Nutcracker".

BIBLE AND NEAR EASTERN MUSEUM

4 - Anderson. Anderson University. 1100 East 5th Street. (765) 643-5633. Artifacts from the Holy Land. History of the Near East as it relates to the Bible.

KOKOMO CIVIC THEATRE FOR CHILDREN
CURTAIN CALL

4 – Kokomo. 320 West Walnut Street. (765) 452-7165.

KOKOMO COMMUNITY CONCERTS

4 – Kokomo. 108 North Main Street. (765) 452-4006.

KOKOMO SYMPHONY ORCHESTRA

4 – Kokomo. 2601 South Webster. (765) 455-1659.

EASTER PAGEANT
Marion Memorial Coliseum, **Marion**

- ❑ **Area: 4**
- ❑ Telephone Number: (765) 664-3947
- ❑ Hours: Good Friday and Easter
- ❑ Admission: No (Except Good Friday)
- ❑ Miscellaneous: The Easter story unfolds in a one-hour performance produced by 2000 volunteers. The Passion story is told entirely in pantomime, pageantry, great anthems and hymns-with no spoken commentary.

MINNETRISTA CULTURE CENTER
1200 North Minnetrista Parkway, **Muncie**

- ❑ **Area: 4**
- ❑ Telephone Number: (765) 282-4848 or (800) 4CULTURE
- ❑ Hours: Tuesday - Saturday, 10:00 am - 5:00 pm
  Sunday, 1 - 5:00 pm

❑   Admission: Adults $5.00, Seniors $3.00, Students $3.00
    (under 12), Family $15.00
❑   Miscellaneous: Gift shop with educational toys and art.
    Summer outdoor concerts. Orchard shop features apples,
    cider, and Indiana-made products through the Fall.

"Minnetrista" means "a gathering place by the water". A series of
impressive large columns greet you at the entrance. They are all
that remains of the F.C. Ball house destroyed by fire in 1967.
Other Ball family homes on the grounds are used for offices and
meetings. Exhibits cover local history, art, science, and industry.
Favorite exhibits usually revolve around lasers, virtual reality, or
hologram displays.

WHITE RIVER YOUTH CHOIR

4 - Muncie. (765) 759-9354.

JUNIOR PLAYERS OF RICHMOND

4 – Richmond. 1003 East Main Street. (765) 962-1816. Produces
drama and theatre arts education for children, by children. Three
times per year.

RICHMOND ART MUSEUM

4 - Richmond. Richmond High School, 350 Hub Etchison
Parkway. (765) 966-0256. Hands-on exhibit entitled "Art is..." for
K-3 grades. Introduces basic art elements of different cultures,
Tuesday - Friday, 10:00 am - 4:00 pm. Saturday & Sunday,
1 - 4:00 pm.

ASANTE CHILDREN'S THEATRE

6 – Indianapolis. Walker Theater. (317) 638-6694. Children (ages
8-18 years) perform original plays centered on African American
culture and current issues. Admission.

BALLET INTERNATIONALE

6 - **Indianapolis**. Clowes Memorial Hall. (317) 637-8979 or Box Office (317) 921-6444. The Nutcracker Christmas Classic.

CARMEL SYMPHONY ORCHESTRA

6 - **Indianapolis**. (317) 844-9717. Family concerts.

CHILDREN OF COLOR FESTIVAL

6 – **Indianapolis.** Broad Ripple, Indianapolis Art Center. (317) 255-2464. One day arts event celebrating diversity of children.

EITELJORG MUSEUM OF AMERICAN INDIAN AND WESTERN ART

500 West Washington Street (White River State Park), **Indianapolis**

- ❑ **Area: 6**
- ❑ Telephone Number: (317) 636-9378
- ❑ Admission. Tuesday - Saturday, 10:00 am - 5:00 pm Sunday, Noon - 5:00 pm
- ❑ Tours: Daily, 2:00 pm

Pottery, basketry, clothing, jewelry, paintings and sculpture of Native American and Western artists. Kids Indian crafts or demonstrations offered. Pick up Family Guide listing of activities and questions to answer. You'll feel you walked into a Santa Fe courtyard as you tour the rooms.

INDIANAPOLIS CHILDREN'S CHOIR

6 - Indianapolis. 4600 Sunset Avenue. (317) 940-9640. 800 children and 12 different choirs perform 50 times a year. "My child is a Children's Choir member" is a popular bumper sticker.

INDIANAPOLIS CHILDREN'S THEATRE

6 – Indianapolis. 5630 East Washington Street. (317) 322 - 1711. Annual series for families. Classes offered.

INDIANAPOLIS JUNIOR CIVIC THEATRE

6 – Indianapolis. 1200 West 38th Street. (317) 924-6770. Box Office, (317) 923 - 4597. 1st – 4th grade productions.

INDIANAPOLIS MUSEUM OF ART

6 – Indianapolis. 38th and Michigan. (317) 923-1331, Tuesday - Saturday, 10:00 am - 5:00 pm. Sunday, Noon - 5:00 pm. Open late on Thursday. Snack area or cafe. Tours daily at Noon and 2:15 pm. Known for Oriental art, "LOVE" prints and sculpture. Free.

INDIANA REPERTORY THEATRE

6 – Indianapolis. 140 West Washington Street. (317) 635-5277. Box Office, (317) 635-5252. Upperstage Family Series. Sunday Matinees.

INDIANAPOLIS SYMPHONY ORCHESTRA

6 – Indianapolis. 45 Monument Circle, Hibert Circle Theatre. Yuletide Celebration concerts. Family series, Symphony on the Prairie Summer outdoor concerts.

NATIONAL ART MUSEUM OF SPORT

6 – Indianapolis. University Place, 850 Michigan Street. (317) 274- 3627. Monday - Friday, 8:00 am - 5:00 pm. Largest display of sports-related fine art. Free.

MELCHIOR MARIONETTE THEATRE

6 - **Nashville**. South VanBuren Street. (800) 849-4853. Outdoor handcrafted marionette shows. (July – October)

MIKE'S MUSIC AND DANCE BARN

6 - **Nashville**. 2277 West SR 46. (812) 988-8636. Non-smoking, non-alcoholic country dance place. Lessons for line dancing. Sandwich/snacks menu. $3 - $6.00 entrance fee.

NATIONAL FOLLIES

6 - **Nashville**. (800) 449-SHOW. $5.00 - $12:00. Various matinee shows, singing, dancing and comedy. (June – December)

PINE BOX THEATRE

6 - **Nashville**. 168 South Jefferson. (800) 685-9624. Sunday Matinee. Oldies music and dance. Meet the performers afterwards. (February – December)

T.C. STEELE STATE HISTORIC SITE

4220 South T.C Steele Road (off SR 4),
Nashville

- ❑ **Area: 6**
- ❑ Telephone Number: (812) 988-2785
- ❑ Hours: Tuesday - Saturday, 9:00 am - 5:00 pm.
  Sunday, 1 - 5:00 pm
- ❑ Admission: Free
- ❑ Miscellaneous: Theodore Clement Steele (1847-1926) noted Indiana artist's home and studio. See exhibits of Impressionistic paintings by the Hoosier Group painter. Surrounding nature preserves provide inspiration.

YOUNG ABE LINCOLN MUSICAL DRAMA

Lincoln State Park Amphitheatre. (I-64, Exit 57 to 231 South), **Lincoln City**

- ❑ **Area: 7**
- ❑ Telephone Number: (800) 264-4223
- ❑ Hours: Tuesday - Sunday, 1:30 pm, CDT and 8:00 pm CDT . Reservations best. (Mid-June - Mid-August)
- ❑ Admission: Adults $12.00, Seniors $10.00 (60+), Children $7.00 (under 13)
- ❑ Tours: Backstage $2.00/person before shows
- ❑ Miscellaneous: "Railsplitter" supper available before performance. Sunday Family Night is $7.00/person. Completely covered amphitheatre. No rainchecks.

S ee the Story of Lincoln's Youth in Southern Indiana. Relive the early 1800's on the Indiana frontier as over 40 actors become (very believable) Lincoln family and friends. See him deal with the death of his mother and sister and his first brush with slavery. Experience the touching, funny and serious sides of youth that developed him into a well respected man.

HOOSIER THEATRE

9 – **Vevay**. 1837 theatre presents live musical and theatre performances in historical setting.

Chapter 9

SPORTS

TobyStarr

- **INDIANA YOUTH BOWLING ASSOCIATION**
  (317) 357-2695
- **INDIANA YOUTH SOCCER ASSOCIATION**
  (317) 255-0499

COLLEGE FOOTBALL HALL OF FAME

111 South St. Joseph Street (Downtown, 2 blocks East of Main Street), **South Bend**

❑ **Area: 1**
❑ Telephone Number: (219) 235-9999, (800) 440 FAME,
   www.college football.org/
❑ Hours: Daily,10:00 am - 5:00 pm (January – May)
   Daily, 10:00 am - 7:00 pm (June – December)
❑ Admission: Adults $9.00, Seniors $6.00,
   Children $4.00 (6-14)
❑ Miscellaneous: Gift shop-logo and autographed items.

- The Locker Room - Walk into a scene where coaches are training and motivating future football heroes. Designed to make you feel you're really being coached.
- Pigskin Pageantry - interactive tribute to the fans, mascots, cheerleaders and marching bands that create the festivity.
- Hall of Champions - photos and momentos.
- Stadium Theater – 360 degree screen theater that puts you in the middle of a game from pre-game cheers, to playing rough on the field, to the victory celebration.
- Training Center – Test YOUR football skills at a series of challenges in passing, running, and kicking.

E ven as you walk up to the building, your kids will have fun playing on the ½ football field entrance (we bought a College Football Hall of Fame football and later played catch on "the turf" outside). See the "Pursuit of a Dream" (college football theme sculpture - 3 stories tall!) that will be reminiscent for any college grad (can you count the # of pizza boxes?).

EAST RACE WATERWAY

1 - South Bend. 301 South St. Louis Boulevard. (219) 284-9401. 2000 ft. artificial whitewater course with canoe and kayak national and international races. (June - Labor Day)

SILVER HAWKS

1 - South Bend. Coveleski Stadium. Class "A" baseball team for the Chicago White Sox.

SOUTH BEND MOTOR SPEEDWAY

1 - South Bend. 25698 State Road. (219) 287-1704. Fridays at 6:00 pm. Demolition Derby, Saturdays at 7:00 pm. Auto stock racing, formula Indy, classic stock, IMCA modified. Admission. (April – September)

FORT WAYNE'S FURY

2 - Fort Wayne. Memorial Coliseum. (219) 483-1111. CBA American Conference Basketball.

KOMETS

2 - Fort Wayne. Memorial Coliseum. (219) 483-1111. IHL team.

MAD ANTHONY GOLF TOURNAMENT

2 - Fort Wayne. (800) 767-7752. Annual "who's who" of Indiana sports and entertainment celebrities play with PGA/LPGA touring pros.

WIZARDS

2 - Fort Wayne. Memorial Stadium. (219) 483-1111. Class "A" field team for Minnesota Twins.

KIL-SO-QUEST SLED DOG RACE

2 - Huntington. Kilso-Quah Campground. (219) 723-6225. Indiana's only sled dog race! 2,3,4 and 6 dog races. No admission. (2nd weekend in January)

GO-KART DIRT RACING

3 - Crawfordsville. Ben Hur Speedway. (765) 942-7903. Year-round races 2 times per month, Saturdays, 7:00 pm.

SUGAR CREEK CANOE RACE

3 – Crawfordsville. Elston Park. (765) 364-0969. Annual 10.5 and 16 mile USCA-sanctioned races; children's events. No admission.

GREAT MILL RACE

3 - Cutler. Adams Mill. (765) 463-7893. 3rd Saturday in July. Boat mill races for fun every half-hour. Food, demonstrations. No Admission.

PURDUE UNIVERSITY ATHLETICS

3 - Lafayette. (765) 494-3194.

ANDERSON SPEEDWAY

4 - Anderson. 1311 Pendleton Avenue. (765) 642-0206. Admission. Saturdays, 8:00 pm (April–October) and Wednesdays, 7:00 pm (June – August)

INDIANAPOLIS COLTS TRAINING CAMP

4 - Anderson. University Track and Field off East 3rd Street. (800) 533-6569. NFL football team pre-season practice. Free. (End of July – August)

MAYOR'S CUP GRAND PRIX KART RACE

4 - **Anderson**. (800) 533-6569. (May)

BROWNSTOWN SPEEDWAY

4 - **Brownstown**. Jackson County Fairgrounds. (888) 524-1914. Stock car races. Saturdays. (March – October)

EVANS KOKOMO SPEEDWAY

4 – **Kokomo**. SR35 North. (765) 459-3877.

SPEED CREEK RACEWAY

4 – **Lapel**. 2620 South, 1000 West. (I-69 and SR 13). (765) 754-7266. Live NasKart racing action. Thursday - Sunday. Admission.

GAS CITY I-69 SPEEDWAY

4 – **Marion**. 5739 East 500 South. (765) 674-6135. Quarter mile dirt track, racing sprints, modified and street stock. Fridays, 7:00 pm. Admission. (May –October)

ACADEMY OF MODEL AERONAUTICS CENTER
5151 East Memorial Drive (SR 67 East [by-pass] to Memorial Exit), **Muncie**

- ❏ **Area: 4**
- ❏ Telephone Number: (765) 287-1256 or (800) 435-9262
- ❏ Hours: Monday - Friday, 8:00 am - 5:00 pm, EST
  Saturday - Sunday, 10:00 am - 4:00 pm
- ❏ Admission: Donation
- ❏ Miscellaneous: Gift Shop with souvenirs plus educational books and kits.

Colorful model planes hang above you as you wander through many well-designed displays that comprise the largest collection of memorabilia and flying models in the world. The types of flying miniature craft include free flight, indoor, control line (lines connect the model and pilot), radio control and scale models. Look close for the plaques identifying world record holders. The 1000 acre exhibit and competition fields showcase the only form of aviation open to everyone. We were there for a rocket launch event.... 3 - 2 - 1 ... *LIFT OFF!* A few moments after lift off, the rocket's parachute floats back to earth. The friendly participants evoke interest in the sport.

ACADEMY OF MODEL AERONAUTICS / HOBBY-SPORT GRAND EVENT

4 – Muncie. 5151 East Memorial Drive. International Aeromodeling Center. (765) 287-1256. Try out model airplanes, boats, cars, rockets, kites and remote-control vehicles on display and for sale. No admission. (2nd weekend of June)

BALL STATE ATHLETICS

4 - Muncie. Ball State University. (765) 285-1474. Mid-American Conference Division I-A.

NATIONAL AEROMODELING CHAMPIONSHIPS

4 - Muncie. 5151 East Memorial Drive. (765) 287-1256. Aeromodel Museum. Largest event in the world with 1200 competitors. 104 separate events. No admission. (Mid-July - Early August)

INDIANA BASKETBALL HALL OF FAME MUSEUM

One Hall of Fame Court (I-70 to SR 3 North Exit [5 miles]), **New Castle**

❑   **Area: 4**
❑   Telephone Number: (765) 529-1891

- ❑ Hours: Tuesday - Saturday, 10:00 am - 5:00 pm
  Sunday, Noon - 5:00 pm
- ❑ Admission: Adults $3.00, Children $1.00 (5-12)
- ❑ Tours: 20+, reduced rates
- ❑ Miscellaneous: Gift Shop. Favorite (and most crowded) time to visit is early Spring for the start of the basketball season called "March Madness".

Hoosier-mania about basketball. Boys and girls high school, college and pro stars with signed balls, jerseys and trophies. $0.25 jump exhibit to test skills against Oscar Robertson. Test your knowledge of basketball trivia on a computer game or pretend you're playing for the winning shot in the final seconds of a game! If you make it, you're awarded a souvenir blue ribbon.

INDIANA FOOTBALL HALL OF FAME

815 North A Street (Downtown, corner of North 9th and "A" streets) **Richmond**

- ❑ **Area: 4**
- ❑ Telephone Number: (765) 966-2235
- ❑ Hours: Monday - Friday, 10:00 am - 4:00 pm
  (May – September). Monday - Friday, 10:00 am - 2:00 pm
  (October - April) Weekends by appointment.
- ❑ Admission: Adults $1.00, Children $0.50 (under 16)
- ❑ Tours: By appointment

High school, college and professional Indiana players. 100 year old football uniforms - see changes in uniforms from the 1890's to present. Star profile exhibits like Purdue's 1967 Rose Bowl Champs, Weeb Ewbanks (coach), Jim Thorpe, Knute Rockne and the famous "Four Horsemen of Notre Dame".

RICHMOND ROOSTERS PROFESSIONAL BASEBALL

4 - Richmond. Don McBride Stadium. (765) 935-7529. Class "A" independent frontier league. Admission. (June – August)

WINCHESTER SPEEDWAY

4 – Winchester. RR 1, SR 32 West. USAC sprints, midget and stock cars (NASCAR) on world's fastest ½ mile banked track.

BLOOMINGTON SPEEDWAY

6 - Bloomington. 5185 South Fairfax Road. (812) 824-7400. Dirt oval track for sprint, open-wheel modified and street stocks. Every other Friday.

INDIANA UNIVERSITY SPORTS

6 - Bloomington. (800) 447-4648. Football, soccer, tennis, swimming, track and field, wrestling and basketball.

LITTLE 500

6 - Bloomington. Indiana University. Made famous by the movie, "Breaking Away". This competitive event features IU's best cyclists at Armstrong Stadium. (April)

HOOSIER HORSE FAIR

6 - Indianapolis. State Fair Event Center. (317) 692-7115. Professional Rodeo. Admission. (April)

HOOSIER STATE GAMES

6 - Indianapolis. (800) HI-FIVES. Qualifications and finals for 15 sports. Includes soccer, volleyball, basketball, swimming, cycling, bowling, wrestling, table tennis, gymnastics. (June – November)

INDIANA PACERS

6 – Indianapolis. Market Square Arena. (317) 639-6411. NBA Basketball. Coached by Hoosier Superstar, Larry Bird.

INDIANA TWISTERS

6 – **Indianapolis**. Market Street Arena. (317) 951-1811. CISL Pro-soccer. (June – September)

INDIANAPOLIS 500 SPEEDWAY RACE

6 – **Indianapolis**. Indy Motor Speedway. (317) 481-8500. Biggest 1-day sporting event in the world! (Memorial Day Weekend)

INDIANAPOLIS COLTS

6 – **Indianapolis**. NFL Football. RCA Dome. (317) 297-7000.

INDIANAPOLIS ICE

6 – **Indianapolis**. Market Square Arena. (317) 639-2112. Top minor-league club of NHL's Chicago Blackhawks.

INDIANAPOLIS INDIANS

6 – **Indianapolis**. Victory Field. (317) 269-3545. Minor-league affiliate of the National League's Cincinnati Reds.

INDIANAPOLIS RACEWAY PARK

6 – **Indianapolis**. 9901 Crawfordsville Road. (317) 291-4090. U.S. National Drag Racing NHRA. Midgets, sprints, USAC Silver Crown. Kroger Speedfest. (Night before the '500)

INDIANAPOLIS SPEEDOME

6 – **Indianapolis**. 802 South Kitley. (317) 353-8206. Stock car and Figure 8 races. (April – September)

INDIANAPOLIS TENNIS CENTER

6 – **Indianapolis**. IUPUI Campus. (317) 278-2100. RCA Championships. US Tennis Association training site.

NASCAR BRICKYARD 400

6 - **Indianapolis**. Indy Motor Speedway. (317) 481-8500.

THE NATATORIUM

6 – **Indianapolis**. Indiana University, 901 West New York Street. (317) 274-3517. Three indoor pools of national and international aquatic events.

THUNDER ON THE OHIO

7 – **Evansville**. Downtown Riverfront. (812) 464-9576. Week of July 4th . See the world's fastest boat race. Admission.

DUBOIS COUNTY DRAGONS

7 - **Huntingburg**. League Stadium (filming site for 1992 movie, "A League of their Own" with Tom Hanks and Geena Davis). (812) 683-4405. Class "A" Baseball. (June - Mid-August)

THUNDER ON THE WABASH BOAT RACES

7 - **Vincennes**. Kimmel Park.

INDIANA GOVERNOR'S CUP REGATTA

9 - **Madison**. Ohio River. (812) 265-5000. 11:00 am - 5:00 pm. Admission. World's fastest boats (over 200 mph!) compete on a 2 ½ mile course. (July 4th weekend)

COLUMBIA YACHT RACE

10 - **Michigan City (Lake Michigan)**. Oldest Yacht Race on Lake Michigan. (June)

Chapter 10

AMUSEMENTS

Toby & Tony &Nichole

ADVENTURELAND AMUSEMENT PARK

Highway 13 North, **North Webster**

❑ **Area: 1**
❑ Telephone Number: (800) 566-2551
❑ Hours: Daily, Noon - 11:00 pm
❑ Admission: $1.50/ride. Children: Packages $9.00 and up. Go Carts, $3.50
❑ Miscellaneous: Large Kiddieland (includes Kiddie Roller Coaster and Bumper Boats), slide, mini-golf, go-karts, playground and Dixie Steamwheeler rides.

FUN SPOT PARK AND ZOO

2365 North Highway 200 West, **Angola**

❑ **Area: 2**
❑ Telephone Number: (219) 833-2972
❑ Hours: Daily, 10:00 am - 10:00 pm
(Memorial - Labor Day)
❑ Admission: Varies each season and with each activity.
❑ Miscellaneous: Their "after-burner" roller-coaster is the largest in Indiana.

COLUMBIAN PARK

1915 Scott Street, Downtown, SR 26, **Lafayette**

❑ **Area: 3**
❑ Telephone Number: (765) 447-9351
❑ Hours: Zoo, 8:00 am - 9:00 pm (Summer)
8:00 am - 4:30 pm (Winter)
❑ Admission: Free. Pool and rides, Small fee, summer only.

It's a zoo, amusement park and pool. The zoo has an aviary, "touch of country" petting zoo and an animal house. In the amusement park, you'll find a merry-go-round, train ride and several adult rides. To cool off, rent a paddle boat on the pond or swim in the 77,000 square foot pool with a 160 foot curved waterslide or the kiddie water playground.

DENTZEL CAROUSEL
1212 Riverside Drive, **Logansport**

- ❑ **Area: 3**
- ❑ Telephone Number: (219) 753-8725
- ❑ Hours: Seasonal
- ❑ Admission: General, 50 cents/ride.
- ❑ Miscellaneous: Early 1900's stationary carousel handcarved by Gustav Dentsel, (regarded finest artist of his kind).

INDIANA BEACH AMUSEMENT
5224 East Indiana Beach Road
(I-65 to US 24), **Monticello**

- ❑ **Area: 3**
- ❑ Telephone Number: (219) 583-4141
- ❑ Hours: Summer hours, 11:00 am - 11 pm.
  (May – September)
- ❑ Admission: General, $1.50 (age 4+) plus Ride Plans, $7.50 - $21.00 (Or $1.50 per ride)
- ❑ Miscellaneous: Camp Resort. Free Parking.

The 1400 acre lake with sandy beach provides a day full of entertainment without an excessive entrance fee. Popular amusements are the "Den of Lost Thieves" and "Hoosier Hurricane" rides along with Kiddieland, an arcade, mini-golf, and mini-train rides. Browse or eat at the Boardwalk and then watch a Water Ski show after you've taken the plunge on the "Big Flush" waterslide. To relax, try a ride on the "Shafer Queen" paddle wheel boat.

OLD INDIANA FUN PARK
Kent Road and 350 West (I-65, Exit 146), **Thorntown**

- ❑ **Area: 3**
- ❑ Telephone Number: (765) 436-7171
- ❑ Hours: Seasonal hours longer in Summer.
  (Mid-May – September)
- ❑ Admission: Call park for updates.
- ❑ Miscellaneous: Bumper cars, roller coaster, arcade and live entertainment.

STORYBOOK VILLAGE AND PETTING ZOO
SR 159, **Dugger**

- ❑ **Area: 5**
- ❑ Telephone Number: (812) 648-2730
- ❑ Hours: Monday – Saturday, 10:00 am - 6 pm. Sunday, Noon - 6:00 pm (Mid-May – October). Weekends only in September/October.
- ❑ Admission: $2.00. (age 2+)
- ❑ Miscellaneous: Fairy tale scenes and characters. Domesticated animals roam the grounds and can be fed and petted. Mini-train rides and miniature golf.

STAR PORT
Circle Centre (49 West Maryland Street), 4th floor.
Indianapolis

- ❑ **Area: 6**
- ❑ Telephone Number: (317) 237-6498
- ❑ Hours: Sunday – Thursday, 11:00 am - 10:00 pm.
  Friday – Saturday, 11:00 am - 11:00 pm.
- ❑ Admission: General, $3.50 per activity.

Virtual theme park on 4th level of Circle Centre Mall features:

- Showscan - motion theater with high speed action
- Virtual Glider - fly over metropolis of the future or the Grand Canyon
- Virtual Reality - combat experience
- Sega City - 60+ arcade games
- Virtual World - virtual multi-player games where you climb into pods to play games

FUN ISLAND MEGAMAZE
I-64 to US 231, **Dale**

- ❑ **Area: 7**
- ❑ Telephone Number: (812) 937-2020
- ❑ Hours: Daily, Memorial - Labor Day. Weekends in Spring and Fall.
- ❑ Admission: Varies with activity.
- ❑ Miscellaneous: 1 mile long mega-maze plus miniature golf and water balloon launches.

HOLIDAY WORLD THEME PARK AND SPLASHIN' SAFARI

7 miles South of I-64 (Exit 63 or Exit 57, Highway 162),
Santa Claus

- ❑ **Area: 7**
- ❑ Telephone Number: (800) GO-SANTA.
  www.holiday world. com
- ❑ Hours: Holiday World opens 10:00 am; Splashin' Safari
  11:00 am. Closing varies by season. (May - October)
- ❑ Admission: General range $16-22.00. (Guests under 54"
  tall and Seniors have lower rates).
- ❑ Miscellaneous: Season passes and 2-day passes save
  money. Charge cards taken.

Holiday World

- Live shows (country, pop, high dive)
- Raving Rapids whitewater rafting ride
- The Raven is one of the world's best coasters
- Frightful Falls log flume ride
- Costumed characters like HOLIDOG and SAFARI
  SAM roam about
- Banshee six story weightlessness ride
- Santa appears daily-look for him mostly in
  Rudolph's Ranch Kiddie Park

Splashin' Safari

- Certified lifeguards oversee fun areas like:

- Monsoon Lagoon-a 12 level interactive area with
  water effects, body slides and the GIANT bucket.
  WATCH OUT!
- Congo River tube float
- Watubee whitewater ride

- Speed slide, wave pool, covered slide
- Crocodile Isle - scaled-down pool and slides

ATLANTIS WATER PARK

515 Mariott Drive (I-65,Stansifer Avenue Exit), **Clarksville**

- ❑ **Area: 8**
- ❑ Telephone Number: (812) 284-5990
- ❑ Hours: Daily, 10:00 am - 8:00 pm (11:00 am Friday and Saturday).
  (Memorial Day Weekend - Labor Day Weekend)
- ❑ Admission: $10 - $15.00, (Ages 4+)
- ❑ Miscellaneous: Gift Shop, Video Arcade, Tube Rental, Picnic Area (outside Park), Bath House, Sunbathing Deck plus shade available. Concessions.

Tsunami Sea Wave Pool with diamond and roller waves simulate the ocean. Mt. Olympus water slides with ¼ mile of tubing slides. King Neptune's Cove Kiddie Pool (40" height or less only) with triple dolphin slide, giant whale slide, whale crawl, rainmakers and seahorse and tortoise slides.

RIVER FAIR FAMILY FUN PARK

SR 131 (I-65 Exit 4, River Falls Mall, 2nd Floor), **Clarksville**

- ❑ **Area: 8**
- ❑ Telephone Number: (812) 284-3247
- ❑ Hours: Daily, during Mall hours.
- ❑ Admission: Ride passes range from $4 -$10.00
- ❑ Miscellaneous: Indoor amusement park with a carousel, bumper cars, mini-train, mini-golf and a video arcade.

WALLY WORLD FAMILY FUN CENTER
SR 101 (Next to Whitewater State Park), Liberty

- **Area: 9**
- Telephone Number: (765) 458-7229
- Hours: Daily, 10:00 am - 10:00 pm. (Summer) Weekends (April, May, September, October)
- Admission: Varies with game.
- Miscellaneous: Go-cart Tracks, Boat and Tank Tag, Mini-Golf, Kiddy Bumper Boats, Super 93' Dry Slide, Batting Cages, Moon Walks, Train Ride, Basketball, Game Room.

DEEP RIVER WATERPARK
US 30 (off I-65), Merrillville

- **Area: 10**
- Telephone Number: (800) WAV-PARK
- Hours: Memorial Day - Labor Day
- Admission: Average $10.00, General (ages 4 +)
- Miscellaneous: Wave Pool, Tube Slide, Body Slide, Paddles Playland, "Bayou River" ride, "The Storm" tunnel tube ride

SPLASH DOWN DUNES WATER PARK
150 East US 20 (1 mile South of The Indiana Dunes State Park), Porter

- **Area: 10**
- Hours: Daily, 10:00 am - 6:00 pm (Summer). Weekends in September.
- Admission:$9 - $10.00 range. Children 3 and under free.

❑   Miscellaneous: Gift shop and arcade. Concessions.

Giant Twister is a series of 11 slides all twisting by each other;
The Tower – Indiana's tallest slide is 68'; Big Wave is the
Midwest's largest wave pool; Sandcastle Bay - Kids "hang out" for
little ones under 4 feet tall including shorter, wider slides.

<u>NOTES</u>

NOTES

NOTES

NOTES

NOTES

Attention Parents:

(Please pass this page on to a friend)

KIDS ♥ INDIANA ™

❖ **Discover places where you can "co-star" in a cartoon or climb a giant sand dune.** You'll find listings on well-known attractions plus tours and special events you probably never thought of .

❖ **A wonderful resource to make short vacation plans or get to know your hometown area better.** You will probably find there are at least 50 things to do within an hour of your home! Almost 600 listings in one book about Indiana travel for kids ages 2 – 15!

❖ **Kid-Tested.** We personally visited all of the most unique places. Written with warmth and excitement from a parent's perspective. Tried and true places that children enjoy. No more boring trips.

❖ **Formatted in 10 geographical zones** providing addresses, telephone numbers, directions, and descriptions.

❖ **Save Time.** We spent over 1000 hours doing all of the scouting, collecting and compiling so that you could spend less time searching and more time having fun!

❖ **Great tool for moms, dads, grandparents, teachers, babysitters and visitors** to plan exciting days all around Indiana.

❖ **Save Money.** We have found lots of places to visit for little or no charge!

Name_____

Address_____

City_____

State_____Zip_____

*Enclose check or money order payable to **KIDS LOVE PUBLICATIONS** and send to:*

KIDS LOVE PUBLICATIONS
7438 Sawmill Road, PMB 500
Columbus, Ohio 43235
(614) 898-2697
www.kidslovepublications.com

Quantity	Price (ea)	TOTAL
	$12.95	$
Shipping		**FREE**
Sales Tax	Ohio Residents Only	($0.75) each
TOTAL		

Attention Parents:

(Please pass this page on to a friend)

KIDS ♥ PENNSYLVANIA ™

- ❖ **Explore places where you "discover" oil, meet Ben Franklin, or watch your favorite toys being made.** Well-known attractions plus tours & special events you probably never knew.

- ❖ **Wonderful resource to make short vacation plans or get to know your hometown area better.** You will probably find there are at least 100 things to do within an hour of your home! Nearly 1000 listings in one book about Pennsylvania travel for kids ages 2 – 15!

- ❖ **Formatted in 9 geographical zones** providing addresses, telephone numbers, directions, and descriptions to save you lots of time!

- ❖ **Great tool for moms, dads, grandparents, teachers, babysitters and visitors** to plan exciting days all around Pennsylvania. Kid-tested!

- ❖ **Economy.** We have found lots of places to visit for little or no charge!

BOOK AVAILABLE APRIL 1, 2000

Name _____

Address _____

City _____

State _____ Zip _____

www.kidslovepublications.com

*Enclose check or money order payable to **KIDS LOVE PUBLICATIONS** and send to:*

KIDS LOVE PUBLICATIONS
7438 Sawmill Road, PMB 500
Columbus, Ohio 43235
(614) 898-2697

Quantity	Price (ea)	TOTAL
	$12.95	$
Shipping	Sales Tax	**FREE**
Sales Tax	Ohio Residents Only	($0.75) each
TOTAL		

GROUP DISCOUNTS AND FUNDRAISER OPPORTUNITIES!

Dear Coordinator:

We're excited to introduce our new book to your group! This new guide for parents, grandparents, teachers and visitors is a great tool to discover hundreds of fun places to visit around Indiana. **KIDS ♥ INDIANA** is one resource for all the wonderful places to travel either locally or across the state.

We are two parents who have researched, written and published this book. We have spent over 1000 hours collecting information and, very often, visiting every site listed in this guide. This book is kid-tested and the descriptions include great hints on what kids like best!

After you have reviewed your copy of **KIDS ♥ INDIANA**, please consider the following options:

- ❑ **Group Discount/Fundraiser** – Purchase the book at the price of $10.00 and offer the 23% savings off the suggested retail price to members/ friends. Minimum order is ten books. Greater discounts (up to 38%) are available for fundraisers. Call for details.

- ❑ **Available for Interview/Speaking** – The authors have a treasure bag full of souvenirs from favorite places in Indiana. We'd love to share ideas on planning fun trips to take children while exploring Indiana. The authors are available, by appointment, at (614) 898-2697. The minimum guaranteed order is 50 books. There is no additional fee involved.

Call us soon at (614) 898-2697 to make arrangements!
Happy Exploring!

Attention Parents:

(Please pass this page on to a friend)

KIDS ♥ OHIO ™

❖ **Discover places like hidden castles and whistle factories.** You'll find listings on well-known attractions plus tours and special events you probably never thought of .

❖ **A wonderful resource to make short vacation plans or get to know your hometown area better**. You will probably find there are at least 100 things to do within an hour of your home! Nearly 1000 listings in one book about Ohio travel for kids ages 2 – 15!

❖ **Kid-Tested**. We personally visited all of the most unique places. Written with warmth and excitement from a parent's perspective. Tried and true places that children enjoy. No more boring trips.

❖ **Formatted in 9 geographical zones** providing addresses, telephone numbers, directions, and descriptions.

❖ **Save Time.** We spent over 1000 hours doing all of the scouting, collecting and compiling so that you could spend less time searching and more time having fun!

❖ **Great tool for moms, dads, grandparents, teachers, babysitters and visitors** to plan exciting days all around Ohio.

❖ **Save Money.** We have found lots of places to visit for little or no charge!

Name_____

Address_____

City_____

State_____Zip_____

www.kidslovepublications.com
Enclose check or money order
*payable to **KIDS LOVE**
PUBLICATIONS and send to:*

KIDS LOVE PUBLICATIONS
7438 Sawmill Road, PMB 500
Columbus, Ohio 43235
(614) 898-2697

Quantity	Price (ea)	TOTAL
	$12.95	
Shipping		FREE
Sales Tax	*(Ohio Residents)*	($.75) ea
TOTAL		$

Attention Parents:
(Please pass this page on to a friend)

KIDS ♥ MICHIGAN ™

- ❖ **Discover places where you can "race" over giant sand dunes, climb aboard a lighthouse "ship", or watch your favorite foods being made.** Well-known attractions plus tours & special events you probably never knew.

- ❖ **Wonderful resource to make short vacation plans or get to know your hometown area better.** You will probably find there are at least 50 things to do within an hour of your home! Over 700 listings in one book about Michigan travel for kids ages 2 – 15!

- ❖ **Formatted in 8 geographical zones** providing addresses, telephone numbers, directions, and descriptions to save you lots of time!

- ❖ **Great tool for moms, dads, grandparents, teachers, babysitters and visitors** to plan exciting days all around Michigan. Kid-tested!

- ❖ **Economy.** We have found lots of places to visit for little or no charge!

BOOK AVAILABLE APRIL 1, 2000

Name_____

Address_____

City_____

State_____Zip_____

www.kidslovepublications.com
*Enclose check or money order payable to **KIDS LOVE PUBLICATIONS** and send to:*

KIDS LOVE PUBLICATIONS
7438 Sawmill Road, PMB 500
Columbus, Ohio 43235
(614) 898-2697

Quantity	Price (ea)	TOTAL
	$12.95	$
Shipping	Sales Tax	**FREE**
Sales Tax	Ohio Residents Only	($0.75) each
TOTAL		